RURAL
CHURCH
ADMINISTRATION

RURAL

CHURCH

ADMINISTRATION

Rockwell C. Smith

ABINGDON-COKESBURY PRESS
New York   •   Nashville

RURAL CHURCH ADMINISTRATION

Copyright MCMLIII by Pierce & Washabaugh

Library of Congress Catalog Card Number: 53 5402

SET UP, PRINTED, AND BOUND BY THE
PARTHENON PRESS, AT NASHVILLE,
TENNESSEE, UNITED STATES OF AMERICA

In grateful memory of

LISGAR RUSSELL ECKARDT

1876-1946

head of the department of philosophy at DePauw University,
1913-1945, who taught me that in the resolute discovery of
truth and our passionate dependence upon it lie both
freedom and peace

and in affectionate appreciation of his wife

ETHEL WILSON ECKARDT

who has wholeheartedly taken me as a son-in-law into the
household of her concern

PREFACE

THIS VOLUME is designed to serve as a workbook for the town and country church pastor. It is written out of the background of my own experience as rural pastor for twelve years and as teacher of rural churchmanship for another twelve years, during which both students and pastors in the field have shared their experiences with me. What teacher, student, and pastor have learned together is reported with the hope that others will enlarge the scope of the discoveries and test the principles herein set forth.

Such a workbook is characterized by certain limitations. As the reader will note, the treatment is neither complete nor exhaustive; not only is our knowledge incomplete in this field, but there is in existence a whole series of books on church administration to which reference may be made for general principles. In the bibliography are listed a number of books on the subject. Almost two thirds of these have been published in the last decade, over a third of them in the last five years. This book attempts specifically to apply church administration methods to the town and country church; its purpose is supplementary rather than comprehensive.

Procedures suggested in the following pages may be so enthusiastically commended as to give an impression of dogmatism. Let me hasten to assure the reader that these suggestions are developed as *a* way, not *the* way. No exclusive right or authority is claimed for the methods described; while these seem the best available at present, the search for better ones must continue. I hope that the indebtedness to town and country pastors which these pages so obviously show will encourage other pastors to contribute to the search by sharing their own problems and discoveries with their brothers in the field.

These chapters have been made possible by a whole series of influences and events. Recent experiences particularly helpful in my thinking have been associated with participation in the 1950 Bible Week at Bethel College, North Newton, Kansas; the 1951 Home Mission Lectureship at Pittsburgh-Xenia Theological Seminary; the 1951 National Methodist Conference of Town and Country Work; the 1951 Idaho Methodist Pastors' Retreat; and the 1951 United Church of Canada Pastors' School at St. Stephens College, Edmonton, Alberta. To the Interdenominational School for Rural Workers at Garrett Biblical Institute, in which I have been active for twelve summers, I am indebted for the stimulating fellowship with pastors of many denominations.

The time to write these pages I owe to the trustees of Garrett Biblical Institute, who granted me a sabbatical quarter for that purpose. I take this opportunity to express my appreciation for such groups of Christians whose business judgment and acumen and whose generosity of time and talent make theological education possible. To President Horace G. Smith, who first brought me to Garrett and then over the years brought Garrett to me, I am proud to acknowledge my debt of educational philosophy; his insight into what a minister needs to be and the part education plays in making men ministers has constituted throughout my years of teaching both a challenge and an inspiration.

The Rev. and Mrs. Lucian Wilson of the United Student Christian Fellowship at the University of New Mexico discovered the mountain cabin in the Sandias near Albuquerque in which these pages were written. This is but another example of their thoughtful friendship over the years.

My secretary, Miss Vera Largen, has uncomplainingly and efficiently made legible typescript of my scrawled pages; I am deeply appreciative of her patience, dependability, and willingness.

To my wife, Frances, I owe a special debt of gratitude for putting up with my difficult authorship. Patience, humor, and critical literary skill have been her unfailing contributions to what ought to be viewed as a joint project. I say "Thank you" with a prayer that what is here recorded may be worth the sacrifice she made to get it on paper.

ROCKWELL C. SMITH

CONTENTS

The Uniqueness of the
Town and Country Church

THERE ARE many persons who will turn the pages of this book with a question as to whether a book discussing specifically the work of the town and country church is necessary or even advisable. "People are people everywhere," they may observe, "with common needs, common sins, common problems, all best answered and met in the common gospel of Christ." Some will go farther and insist: "To talk of town and country churches and persons as if they are different is to raise dividing lines within the church and to make a rallying center for dissatisfied and unsuccessful preachers who by stressing their rural loyalties hope to secure some personal preferment."

Let us begin by candidly admitting the element of truth in both statements. Persons are persons everywhere, and the gospel is for all men alike. But we shall not deal in these pages with the problems of making the gospel message effective among persons in general. There are areas of life and work in which rural persons face special problems and need particular applications of the gospel message. It is with these that we shall concern ourselves. Red and blue have much in common: they are both colors. But it would be a strange sort of artist indeed who refused to recognize the difference between them or to take account of it in his creations.

It is also true that dissatisfied and unsuccessful men seek to gain personal advancement and security by becoming champions of causes real and imaginary. But their motivation is no condemnation of the cause they support. It is quite possible that their frustration leads to a sensitivity to unmet needs which satisfied and successful men do not have. I do not suggest for a moment that such a motivation exists among rural churchmen. All I am insisting on is that even a clear demonstration of its existence would not absolve us from responsibility for a careful analysis of what such individuals have to say about the peculiar characteristics of the rural church and its people.

What differences exist as between rural and urban people? To begin with we agree that there are no absolute differences between them. Differences which do exist are of a degree. Rural people live and work in a society governed less by the clock and more by the calendar. The regularity of an eight-hour shift is alien to them, though miners and commuters are governed by the time clock. They know seasons of relative leisure and seasons of unrelenting, almost ceaseless, toil. Their society, by and large, is one in which a man knows a small number of people very well indeed; it contrasts with urban society in which a man is interdependent with a vast number of people yet knows most of them either casually or not at all. Rural people participate in groups, each one made up of a limited number of the same people. Urban people participate in many groups, no two of which have the same membership.

"How shall we differentiate rural and urban population in terms of numbers?" you may ask. Well, when it comes to counting we are always in something of a dilemma. The United States census counts everyone living in an incorporated or unincorporated population division of 2,500 or more plus persons living in less populated areas adjacent to cities of 50,000 or more as urban. This definition was first used in the 1950 census and moved a total of 7,500,000 persons from the rural to the urban category. As the census now counts, 63.7 per cent of Americans are urban and 36.3 per cent are rural. The National Council of the Churches of Christ in the U.S.A. sets the dividing line, in relationship to home mission work, at 10,000 population. Work in communities of less than 10,000 is called town and country work. We shall

14

use the church definition in our discussion except at the point of statistics where we have to depend upon census counts. Obviously any merely numerical definition is in particular cases unsatisfactory. We shall be able to take this into account; what is important is to understand what is meant when we use the terms with a numerical connotation.

Rural people are commonly thought of as farmers. No notion could be more misleading. In the 1950 census 15.7 per cent of the population was identified as rural farm; 20.6 per cent was identified as rural nonfarm. That means that in the entire rural population of the country the farmers are in the minority. Nor do these farmers constitute a homogeneous group in the population. They run all the way from the five-acre ranch owner who has an irrigated orange grove in southern California to the wheat farmer of the plains with his thousands of acres or to the ranchman whose cattle graze over a dozen sections. They run from the subsistence farmer of the Ozarks whose primary concern in farming is to raise what his family needs to eat to the commercial one-crop specialist like the cotton farmer whose eye is always on the exchange market.

Rural nonfarmers are likewise a heterogeneous lot. We think quite inevitably of the small town service center and its people when we say rural nonfarm. But coal miners are rural nonfarm, as are oil and gas drillers and well workmen. Commuters from urban employments complicate the picture by the hundred thousands. They live in a rural community and work in a nearby city, and their numbers extend from the city handy man living in his garage or basement while he builds his country home on the installment plan to the president of First National Bank with his palatial estate on the ridge. All are rural nonfarm.

The thoughtful reader may point out that this same heterogeneity is a characteristic of urban life and that our argument as to the difference between urban and rural breaks down at this point. Such a conclusion fails to take into account the situations in which heterogeneity exists. In urban life

15

there are people of very diverse occupational and social interests, but these people exist in such large numbers that they can have separate churches ministering to the several kinds. Here is a workingman's church; here is a mission church in an area of transition where the new migrant to the city begins his urban experience; here is a fashionable church to cater to the country club set. No such easy adjustment to heterogeneity is available to the rural churchmen. Farmer and small town businessman and odd jobs man and urban commuter must all worship together if they are to worship at all. The rural church must deal with diversity not by specialization but by integration.

There are also significant population characteristics in which rural and urban societies differ. Rural society has more men than women; urban society more women than men. In 1950 in all the urban population of the United States there were 94.1 men for every 100 women; in the rural nonfarm population there were 101.3 men per 100 women; in the rural farm population the figure rose to 109.7 men per 100 women. This rural imbalance on the male side is apt to be particularly extreme in the ages between 15 and 35. An effective rural church program must succeed by involving the men, particularly the young unmarried men. A survey of an average Sunday congregation in a rural church will indicate how tragically we miss the mark here.

Rural society has more children than urban society. In 1950 there were 435 children under 5 per 1,000 women 15-44 in our cities, 551 in our rural nonfarm population, and 597 in our rural farm population. Obviously then the reproductive forces of our nation are in its rural people. Over half our children are still in the care of the town and country church, and they must be brought into the Christian fellowship and trained in Christian discipleship before they are sent away to the city for their vocational careers.

And town and country society, particularly its nonfarm segment, has more than its proportionate share of old people. In cities 8.3 per cent of the people were 65 or more in 1950;

16

in the rural farm population 7.4 per cent; but in the rural nonfarm population, 8.3 per cent. These are national figures. In 1940 the rural nonfarm figure was 7.3 per cent, substantially exceeding the urban figure of 6.9 per cent. The increase in the urban figure in 1950 to equal the rural nonfarm is probably due to the new and more inclusive definition of urban. In small town after small town where studies have been made, 16 per cent to 22 per cent 65 years of age and over are the usual figures. These old people represent the richest untapped source of service and leadership which the church has.

We should couple the last two points here to remind ourselves that since the young and old are economically dependent, rural society has a higher proportion of dependents than urban society. That means that fewer workers must support more non-workers in the country than in the city. It also means that the rural church will have fewer incomes to draw upon in the support of its budget for an equal number of persons served. Again here is a peculiar problem of rural church administration. There is a pressing need for the complete exploration and use of the limited financial sources available, and I shall develop a method for such exploration and use in our chapter on the church budget. We have seen thus far that rural society differs from urban in the basic characteristics of its group life, in possessing marked occupational heterogeneity within a small number of people, in the characteristics of the people themselves as far as sex, fertility, and age are concerned. There is yet another significant difference and that is in the church which serves rural society.

Of the 96,000,000 people whom the United States census calls urban, not a single soul is more than three or four miles away at the most from a finely equipped church. Available to him are a beautiful, symbolically rich sanctuary, a series of classrooms for the Christian education of himself and his family, and social rooms for good times and for leisure time activities. On any Sunday morning he can hear a great preacher and study in a church school supervised by a professional, highly trained director of Christian education. If he is in trouble, he can make use of the understanding services of a trained pastoral counselor. Now to say that these services are available to the average city dweller does not mean that he uses them or that if he and his fellow urbanites did use them there would be room and help for all. All that I am saying is that the best religious equipment, personnel, and services are available to the average citizen in the city.

The majority of rural churches, whether in town or open country, are one-room structures. Not only are they minus a specialized ministerial staff, they share the same pastor. They are on circuits of from two to as many as ten churches. This means that the rural pastor in the majority of cases must operate two or more organizational systems. He has two official boards, two women's societies, two church schools, and so on. If his circuit is an exceptionally large one, he may not see some of his congregations more often than once a month. Obviously without the advantage of direct and continually recurring contacts with his people to help him, he must develop a quality of statesmanlike understanding and leadership if he is to do anything more than maintain a precarious ecclesiastical status quo. The more than one third of Americans who are rural must find their religious salvation in an institution and through a pastoral leadership like this.

I have given considerable and detailed attention to this matter of the uniqueness of the rural church problem, because I am convinced that the rural church and the ministry of the general church have been hurt by the easy assumption that urban and rural churches are alike. Many young ministers coming out of seminaries where they have been taught exclusively from the urban point of view (most professors of practical theology are successful former pastors of large city churches) have begun their ministry in rural circuits quite unprepared for the situations they confronted. Confused and hurt by the strangeness of their experiences and the apparent indifference of the people to their message, they have sought a quick and easy transition to urban life; or, failing that,

18

have become permanently embittered men. They have not been given a vision of the rural ministry as a career, and consequently have acquired an element of the breathless and the temporary in their rural pastorates. They have not stayed long enough in a rural parish to develop the personal acquaintance and man-to-man friendliness which rural life requires. By permitting such a state of affairs we have tended to dry up our church life at its roots. Continued neglect of an adequate ministry to our rural people will lead to a more pagan America twenty-five years from now however effective the work we do in the cities may be. Hence a book on rural church administration.

The conscientious reader is by now asking: "Granted all that you say, why is it that sincere church leaders continue to urge that there is no difference between urban and rural church problems and leadership?" An answer to such a question must be speculative of course. Most ministers, church leaders included, begin their ministries in rural churches. Most of us do not do our best at first; we make mistakes, have to learn through costly experience, often end our first pastorate with failure. Most church leaders came to their leadership through pastorates of unusual significance in urban churches. The memory of urban successes is sweet, of rural failure bitter. We are tempted to forget the problem we never did solve by denying its existence and basking in the light of later victories. Hence we say: "People are alike everywhere; there's no difference between urban and rural churches." We as churchmen, and the church itself, will be better off when we realize that there is no shame in failure providing our failure becomes a means of self-exploration, self-understanding, and self-improvement.

In the remaining chapters we shall deal with the problems which are uniquely those of the rural pastor. We will not discuss church administration in general for there already exist excellent books in this field. I shall take it for granted that the reader is familiar with standard works and deal only with such church administration problems and methods as are distinctively of the rural church.

Church administration normally includes the following topics:

> The Minister's Professional Life
> Christian Education
> Community Relationships
> Parish Organization
> Development and Administration of Program
> Leadership in Worship
> Pastoral Duties

Two of these topics will be largely untreated. Christian education is customarily reserved for a separate treatment. A specialized treatment in terms of the rural curriculum is desperately needed but would constitute a work in itself. Herein I shall refer to Christian education only in its relationship to the overall administration of the parish. Community relationships have been dealt with at length in my book, *The Church in Our Town*. A single chapter will discuss the minister's professional life. Much of the material ordinarily dealt with under this heading is common to both urban and rural ministries.

All but the first three chapters of this book will discuss the last four topics, for it is in them that the peculiar circumstances governing rural churchmanship come to play. Even here the discussion will be selective, seeking to supplement the specialized treatments of these matters already current. For example, in dealing with pastoral work we shall largely devote ourselves to its organization within the rural parish. The actual content of various types of calling and counseling have had excellent and comprehensive treatment in other books, some of which are listed in the bibliography.

The reader may notice that the topic of evangelism is missing from the above list. This is not due to any failure to appreciate the evangelistic responsibility of the Christian fellowship but rather to an insistence that a Christian church at every moment and in every action is engaged in the evangelistic enterprise. The making of evangelism a department of church life has been one of the banes of modern Protestantism. We now know that every moment is a moment of decision for or against Christ and that every act of the church should invite and prescribe a Christian commitment to those both within and without its fellowship.

There are several excellent modern treatises on evangelistic methods to which the reader will find references in the bibliography; but let us remember the evangelistic challenge to share the good news in every phase of the church's program.

2

The Town and Country Minister

IN ANY CHURCH the minister is a key figure, but in the town and country church he assumes special importance because the institutional framework of that church is generally so limited. He therefore needs all the qualifications and training of a minister anywhere plus more of intelligence and imagination if possible. It is sometimes assumed that the rural pastor does not need the same rigorous training as his urban colleague since he has to deal with "simple" people. Actually he needs more and better training since he is much more on his own than the urban pastor. Furthermore, in many rural churches he will face Sunday after Sunday a congregation in which numbers of the adults are college graduates. The county agent, the Smith-Hughes agriculture teachers, the Soil Conservation Service specialists, the high-school teachers, the doctors, and the lawyers, not to forget the agriculture college graduate now farming the home place—all are highly educated persons who call out the best in a preacher and pastor.

It is sometimes urged that a town and country pastor needs to have been reared in the country and preferably on a farm. This is highly questionable. Some of our best town and country pastors are city born and bred. Often the farm-reared ministerial candidate has an overestimation of his knowledge of country life. Rural life seems very simple and plain to him whereas in point of fact it is changing and complicated. The average city boy, on the other hand, realizes he doesn't know anything about rural life and wants to learn. That last fact is his salvation. What is important is not a man's place of birth but being open-minded and willing to learn.

The man who is willing to learn can find abundant opportunities. Iowa State College at Ames has a summer-school course in which a theologue may take six weeks of classwork in rural sociology and agricultural economics and six weeks of actual field work in which he lives and works on a farm under the supervision of college personnel. Agricultural colleges even offer a pretheological major for ministerial students which has been accredited for admission by the majority of American theological schools.

All ministers are under bond not only to live exemplary moral lives but to observe special ethical standards in relationship to their own profession. These ministerial ethics are no different for the rural pastor than the urban; hence we shall not give them detailed treatment here. But we must point out that a minister's failure to live up to personal and professional moral standards is more clear and hence more deadly in rural than in urban life. In the city the departmentalization of contacts and relationships permits a minister to depart from the moral code and still maintain some influence and respect among his parishioners, because they are not aware of his total life. No such deception of his flock is possible to a rural pastor; they know him, and that early in his ministry, for what he really is. The man who intends to preach one thing and practice another had better stay out of the town and country church.

The rural pastor generally lives on a low salary compared to his urban colleague. Supervisory officials often seek to point out that salaries are more adequate than they appear because costs of living are lower in rural areas and the minister receives many gifts in kind. Both of these arguments are generally spurious. Our nation is now bound together in a single economy, and prices tend everywhere to be substantially the same. Indeed, since rural merchandizing methods quite generally lag behind urban, the economies of large-scale supermarkets are often not available to the rural pastor; if available, the fact that some independent merchant is a loyal member of the church may make it impolitic to take advantage of them. While it is true that country people do bring to the parsonage

23

gifts in kind from time to time, there is no guarantee that the gifts will be needed or even useful. The young pastor and his wife who in three days time got over ten pounds of pork liver from various neighbors who were butchering is an illustration of the pastor's difficulty with such gifts. Because of their unpredictability as to amount, kind, and timing, such gifts are not a substantial increase to a low salary. Where, as in some sections of north Iowa, the church rents a locker for the pastor in the freezer plant, and people put fruit, vegetables, and meat in his locker as they fill their own, such gifts may be a significant help.

Of course the rural pastor can till a large garden and keep a cow and chickens. Unfortunately many otherwise excellent pastors are neither good nor enthusiastic gardeners. If they garden simply from necessity, the results are apt to be unprofitable both to larder and disposition. Enthusiastic gardeners may be tempted to spend time needed for other duties in the garden, so that parishioners begin to say: "He spends his time gardening when he should be calling on the sick." Whether the charge is justified or not is immaterial; that it is made has already hurt the minister's influence.

It is sometimes suggested that an open-country pastor might well combine farming with the care of a small church. Where this combination comes as a divine calling to a man, we honor him for it. Russell Hoy of Coshocton, Ohio, has made a unique contribution to his neighborhood church and the larger religious life of his community and state by following such a plan. But the success of a single genius is no basis for prescription for pastors in general. Actually farming is a highly skilled profession in our day; and the chances that a man will possess the abilities and disposition to make for success in both farming and the ministry are small. It does not dignify either farming or the ministry to speak as if they could be combined so readily. The Brethren and the Mennonites, churches historically given to a farmer-preacher ministry, are rapidly moving over to a full-time professionally trained ministry.

The rural minister must be prepared, at least for a time,

to work for a salary that is too low. We shall see in our discussion of church finance that more adequate stewardship on the local church level can remedy that situation in part. But a fair salary for rural ministers in general waits upon collective action on the part of denominations. A reduction in the number of competing churches and an economical redistricting of charges are essential to adequate ministerial support for rural churches. For example, the adoption of the basic salary plan outlined in the 1952 *Discipline of The Methodist Church,* paragraph 827, would place the support of the whole ministry on all the churches, which seems fair in the light of the benefit which all churches gain from the work of each pastor in a society as mobile as our own.

Almost always in addition to his cash salary the rural pastor will be supplied with a parsonage. The term does not at present describe a standardized item of housing. Many parsonages are comfortable and commodious homes on which the love of the families of a parish has been expended; others are inadequately designed, indifferently built, and inefficiently maintained dwellings. The Michigan Annual Conference of the Methodist Church has set up a minimum standard for parsonage housing and equipment, as follows:

I. We recommend that the following basic items be completed in each parsonage by Conference time in 1949:
   1. An adequate heating plant.
   2. Adequate cooking facilities.
   3. Electric or gas refrigeration.
   4. Floor coverings on all unusual and non-standard-shaped rooms.
   5. Complete curtains, drapes, and shades for all windows.
   6. Adequate bathroom facilities, with hot and cold water.
   7. Adequate laundry facilities.
   8. Adequate garage space, with a minimum of 10x22 feet.
   9. Sufficient screen for windows.
   10. A lawnmower, rake, spade, hoe, snowshovel, coal shovel, and adequate garden hose.

II. We further recommend that as soon as it is possible, each parsonage be completed in the following respects:
1. A fully equipped utility room.
2. An adequate Church Office and Pastor's Study.
3. Soft water, or a water softener.
4. Sufficient storm windows.
5. Adequate clothes closet and storage space.
6. An adequately insulated house.

III. We suggest that whenever remodeling programs in parsonages are considered that the help of the Methodist Bureau of Architecture, or the Bureau of Architecture of the Home Missions Council or some other competent authority be secured.

Other church bodies might consider the enactment of such a standard. When a parsonage is so built and equipped that it may be well and economically heated in winter, when the kitchen sink and work spaces are of a height congenial to the comfort of a wife at work, when the laundry space and equipment are adequate to the task of keeping the family clothing clean, then a small salary may be wisely and profitably expended. The first goal for ministerial support in a town and country charge should be a modern and efficient parsonage.

In addition to salary and parsonage the rural minister ought to have an expense account. This account should include amounts for stationery and mailing expenses, a part at least of the telephone expense, and an allowance for automobile transportation. An automobile is a necessity in the modern rural parish. The very fact that the minister has several churches assigned to him miles apart underlies the expectation that he will own and use a car. A car is not the minister's private convenience but as much a tool of his work as the church building in which he preaches or the Bible from which he reads. Recently several larger denominational bodies have been experimenting with mileage allowances to pastors. Sometimes the minister has been given a lump sum outright for car expense. This is quite untenable from any reasonable point of view. An expense account is to pay expenses and should be tendered only for expenses incurred.

The lump sum procedure has led certain supervisors to suggest to pastors that they encourage the parish to do away with the expense allowance and to add that sum to the salary. The argument is that with the added sum a man will be in a position to move to another parish at a financial advantage because his stated salary is higher. I point out in passing that from the ethical point of view this represents a misrepresentation and fraud on a man's successor and the parish to which a man goes. Beyond the ethical objection there is an economic one; to add travel expense to the minister's salary as an increase in salary is to obscure the costs of church administration and give a false picture to the parish of the resources the minister has for the care of his family and himself.

Properly each church should set aside an amount for transportation which shall be paid to the minister at so much per mile on receipt by the church treasurer of an itemized monthly statement of miles driven in the work of the church. Six or seven cents a mile is a reasonable figure now, but the actual figure should be revised from year to year. The pastor's monthly bill for mileage serves as an excellent educational device for informing his board of what he is actually doing. After each day's mileage he can put a short identifying statement suggesting the purpose and destination of this or that trip. As his trips to hospitals, public homes, mental and correctional institutions continue to pile up, lay folk begin to see the broadness and the depth of pastoral service.

Sometimes a pastor argues: "I do more driving than the churches will pay me for, anyhow. Why itemize it? I'll take whatever lump sum they give me and let it go at that." First of all, the statement is often just not true. Men think that they drive farther and do more than they actually do. Keeping track of their actual performance is a valuable corrective for them. But if the statement is true, it still does not indicate that an itemized statement and a mileage payment are not important. On the contrary, it is important to local people to know that they are not allowing their pastor enough money to do the work that has to be done. They can scarcely be expected to allow more until they become aware of the inadequacy of their current budget allotment.

Many ministers augment their cash salaries by fees they receive for such special services as funerals, weddings, and baptisms. A word about the fee practice is therefore in order here. Nothing does more psychologically to keep the rural pastor's salary low than the practice of giving him funeral and other fees. Rural parishioners always overestimate the amount of income thus available to him and feel justified in paying a low salary because of their overestimation. Furthermore, the occasional Christian gives the minister ten dollars on the occasion of his wife's funeral and feels that he has behaved handsomely toward religion, the church, and the parson. Since this ten dollars is his only gift to the church, it must be prorated over the twenty years of his wife's life, so that his giving to organized religion on that basis is less than one cent a week. Any practice that develops and maintains such a stewardship of money is fundamentally un-Christian if not anti-Christian.

In this connection we ought to mention that the fee system detracts from the dignity of the ministry and intrudes a financial consideration into relationships with mourners and bereaved that is embarrassing and a handicap to pastoral efficiency. Let the minister once and for all forego such fees and make that known to his people with the expectation that they will pay him a salary adequate to the services he is required to perform and the position he is expected to maintain. In referring to fees it should be explicitly stated that we mean sums of money given to the pastor by families in his parish for the discharge of such ministerial functions as baptizing children, marrying couples, and burying the dead. Honoraria received on the occasion of giving a graduation address or speaking at the Soil Conservation District banquet are quite properly accepted by the pastor.

There are certain nonmaterial rewards and services which

may or may not be available to the town and country minister. Schools for his children are one such social service. Until very recently rural schools have been markedly inferior to urban schools in equipment, curriculum, and personnel. Many fine young pastors have accepted appointment or call to an urban church solely to secure adequate education for their growing children. With the desire to give our children the best training available we cannot but agree. But what we desire for our own children, we ought as Christians to desire for every child. To leave a country church to improve our own children's schooling is to leave the other children exactly in the situation we think not good enough for our own. Should we not rather see the strategic importance of good schooling for all children and become ceaseless fighters for better schools for all the children in our rural community? In *The Church in Our Town* suggestions are given of ways in which rural education may be understood and improved.

A similar situation exists with regard to such other cultural institutions as museums, libraries, and art galleries. These exist almost totally in urban settings. But that does not mean that our children and their friends cannot have the advantage of them. Here the situation is quite different than it is with schools. Pilgrimages can be made by car or bus to outstanding cultural exhibits in urban centers. The minister can encourage this in connection with the public school program and may take his own youth group on such pilgrimages from time to time.

On the other hand there are certain gains for the minister's children in a town and country church setting. Here the active boy and girl may find a wide scope for learning by doing. Pets are not the nuisance and problem they are in the city. The care of rabbits, poultry, a 4-H Club calf or pig becomes an introduction to the biological and economic worlds as well as the means of developing habits of responsibility. Days spent on the farms of school chums lead to the easy familiarity with machinery which is the heritage of the modern farm boy and girl. All these opportunities are the unique possession of the family of the town and country minister.

I have gone to some length in describing the material and nonmaterial recompense that a town and country pastor may expect. All this is not to say that a man should accept or reject a rural charge on these grounds alone. Rather it is important that a man and his wife know what to expect on the salary side to avoid possible disappointment and frustration. The true call of the countryside lies in the men and women, the boys and girls, who are there and who so readily respond to the gospel message.

Four years ago a young man went to a neglected five point circuit. In the intervening years the membership of that circuit has almost tripled. Furthermore, the county in which the churches are located now has a new fifty-bed hospital, a County Health Council, and a Soil Conservation District. These were not all the work of one preacher, but they represent the stimulation and encouragement that he succeeded in bringing to a host of people in the county. Because of his ministry people are alive today who would otherwise have been dead, farmers who saw their land rapidly eroding beneath them now have new vision and new techniques and a consequent higher level of living, the troubled of mind have a comforter and counselor, and the gospel of Jesus is a powerful reality moving in the lives of men and women.

In the light of this experience we cannot but be reminded of our Lord's words to the disciples of John: "Go and shew John again those things which ye do hear and see: The blind receive their sight, and the lame walk, the lepers are cleansed, and the deaf hear, the dead are raised up, and the poor have the gospel preached to them" (Matt. 11:4-5).

3

The Minister's Schedule

A SCHEDULE is important for any minister; for the town and country minister it is essential. The circuit pastor with two or three churches finds innumerable details on his hands and a dozen auxiliary organizations continually clamoring for attention. Unless he carefully schedules his work week, he will find himself totally enmeshed in these details and in the affairs of church auxiliaries, and demonstrating a very shallow ministry indeed. He will be busy, undeniably busy, with many details still neglected, but he will be missing the matters of key importance to his ministry because there is no person or group to clamor for attention to them.

To have a schedule, however, does not mean to be rigid and inflexible in using it. A rural pastor's schedule should keep in mind the facts of the calendar as well as of the day and week. We may plan to call on certain afternoons of the week; but there are seasons of the year when no farm family will welcome a pastoral call because of the pressure of agricultural work. Similarly we must keep in mind the habits of social participation which govern our people. In many rural areas Saturday afternoon is the time when everyone goes to town. There is point in the pastor doing his own trading then or simply walking along Main Street or around the square to meet and greet his parishioners as they visit with their neighbors and friends. Again most rural communities are extremely proud of their high-school basketball teams. Basketball is a game in which a small school can excel. The pastor's schedule should make room for home games at least; it may be good tactics as well as good sport to fill the car with young people and follow the team as it invades alien territory. What we have to say

31

about a schedule should be read in the light of such flexibility.

A first item for any schedule is the minister's own private devotions. Family devotions aside, the minister should have a time for personal prayer and meditation each day. The fact that we ministers lead others in prayer often tempts us to feel that we do not need to pray. The minister who neglects the devotional reading of the Bible and prayer quickly loses that liaison with Heaven which governs a fruitful ministry. Fifteen minutes is certainly a minimum for such practice. Some men prefer the early morning hour for their devotions; others place their period of prayer at the end of the morning study hours so that their study may be summarized and directed by God; others make their devotions at the end of the day, resting their labors in the divine care. Each minister must reach his own decision as to the time and place depending upon his temperament, family situation, and other duties. What we insist upon here is that the devotional life must have its time period in each day's schedule.

The town and country minister works among an early rising people; he will find it advisable to rise no later than 6:30 and be through breakfast and at work by eight in the morning. This allows him time for making himself presentable as well as for breakfast. Some of us develop the bad habit of not shaving and dressing before we go to our studies. In town and country where interruptions are almost certain, this is an exceptionally bad habit. The farm visitor who finds his pastor unshaven and wearing dressing gown and pajamas at ten in the morning will leave with the conviction that he got the pastor out of bed. By eight the pastor should not only be ready for work but dressed and groomed for meeting his people.

Someone is sure to question at this point: "What about time for chores and helping the wife around the house?" Every minister faces this problem, but the rural parsonage with limited equipment places a special burden on the pastor. Some chores like shoveling the walks clear after a snow are occasional and must be cared for at once though they intrude on time otherwise scheduled. Many chores, however, can be anticipated and planned for so as to leave morning hours free for study. Many men find late afternon a good time for lawnmowing and the like. They are then mentally and nervously tired from the pastoral duties of the day and find moderate physical exercise in such routine tasks relaxing and restorative. There are some household duties in which a husband needs to help his wife. These should be understood between the two and planned for in advance so that they can be handled at one time and interfere as little as possible with the professional schedule. Sickness in the family changes the pattern, of course, and requires that the husband do anything and everything he can. Many of us begin our ministries at the same time that we begin our families; hence, we develop bad schedule habits because of the necessarily frequent interruptions young children in the family occasion. The young minister will develop proper habits if he remembers that these early irregularities of schedule are exceptions and does not allow them to become the rule.

The morning hours from eight to twelve should be given over to study. The first two are best devoted to serious and systematic study of the various fields of knowledge. General study is peculiarly important to the rural pastor, since he lacks the stimulus of papers and lectures available in the city and since he will be expected to give a broader community leadership than his urban brother. Let each man make his own division of studies such as the following: theology and philosophy; Bible and church history; ethics and social ethics; psychology, counseling, and Christian education; sociology and community studies; ecumenics, missions, and evangelism. Then let him list under each head volumes he wishes to read and topics he wishes to explore. It is often helpful to be reading on related topics concurrently. The pastor may use his two hours on Tuesday morning for readings in theology and philosophy, for example; on Wednesday morning for psychology, and so on. Over a two-week period he can cover all aspects of his field of study.

Following his two hours of general study, the average minister will want to make a break. It is helpful to many to give over the next half hour to correspondence and other office duties. Then the last hour and a half can be given directly to sermon and worship preparation. Thus the force and content of our general studies are readily available both as stimulus and as development and illustration in our preaching program. The man whose study is exclusively homiletical will increasingly become occasional and topical. The man who gives himself to systematic study will find the very discipline of that study bring unity and integration to all his preaching.

Let a man follow this program Tuesday through Friday. One day of the week, preferably Monday but certainly some specific day, he should take for his day off. The early morning hours on Saturday may be used for study, but in the average rural community Saturday is the day for coming to town and the minister will want to take advantage of this fact to make contacts with his parishioners. It may be objected that this program provides for only sixteen hours of study during the week and that this is not enough. With that criticism I would readily agree but counter with the observation that sixteen hours a week is more than most pastors now spend in regular and disciplined study. This is a minimum. The man of studious habits will quickly find ways to expand that minimum. But unless he develops studious habits through some such scheme, he will do far less than the sixteen hours yet always feel rushed in what study he does.

In this connection the rural minister should consider his subscriptions to scholarly journals. Minimum resources are *Religion in Life* and *Rural Sociology*. The first of these provides cultural and scholarly papers in religion and theology; the second offers research in rural life and values. The book reviews in these two journals will guide his purchases or borrowings, and their articles will raise current academic issues and suggest the manner and method of scholarly research. They will introduce a hard structure of logic into his thinking and preaching in a day when sentimentalism in religion is the bane of the pulpit.

In widely scattered sections of the country rural pastors are developing group approaches to study. The simplest of these is a book and journal circle in which each pastor purchases a new book and subscribes to a current journal, and then these purchases are shared around the circle of those co-operating. Other pastors are meeting at biweekly or monthly intervals on their day off. The meetings are often familial affairs with wife and children coming along for social stimulus and fun. The pastors agree on one of their number who will present a paper on some predetermined subject, and the others come prepared to criticize and discuss. Within group ministries this pattern has proved particularly helpful. Such a program does much to alleviate the circumstances of isolation and intellectual parochialism under which so many town and country pastors are forced to serve.

The afternoons of the rural minister, as of ministers in general, should be reserved for calling and other pastoral work. Circuit ministers find it helpful in expending their time fairly with their several congregations to set apart specific days of the week for individual churches. Then people can leave messages of need at the country store or one of the homes knowing that the pastor will pick them up and respond to them on a given day. This does not mean that emergencies should wait for that particular day; but it is surprising how many times a problem can and will wait for a predetermined time if people know exactly what that time is. The detail of planning the calling in a parish we will deal with when we come to our chapters on the rural pastorate. Here we are only concerned to point out the place of calling in the over-all schedule a minister follows.

Circuit ministers are plagued with evening responsibilities. Night after night they must be away from home for a variety of committee, board, club, and auxiliary meetings. Many of them report that they have not had an undisturbed night at home with the family in a month. This is not a matter which the minister can cure in his own scheduling alone. We shall see when we come to our discussion of church programs that there are means of concentrating meetings on certain nights. What the minister can do in the beginning is to try to limit his evening engagements to not more than four a week, including Sunday evening. The remaining three evenings are reserved for family fellowship and recreation. If these are planned for ahead of time, it is relatively easier to keep evenings free. The last minute request for a committee meeting on Friday night can then be dealt with by saying, "We've invited guests in for dinner and the evening, and I just can't have a meeting then."

In keeping to a schedule, a system of priorities helps to set a standard by which we can depart from or cling to our prior plan. Most pastors would agree that pastoral help in sickness, trouble, death, and bereavement takes precedence over all other duties. When the call comes to attend the sick or dying then all else must stand aside. Next in importance are the worship and preaching services of the church. Not only is it important that we should be prompt in our attendance thereupon, but also that we should be prepared therefor. Study and preparation for worship and preaching should come before everything else except the care of the sick and troubled. Third in the succession of importance are our community responsibilities. To work with other churches and churchmen and such other agencies of the common life as the schools, the farmer and labor organizations, the Extension Service, and health and welfare services is a duty of the pastor. Some would put attention to the administrative details of parish life before community responsibilities, but I would put the church organization last. And I base this order on Jesus' word: "He that findeth his life shall lose it: and he that loseth his life for my sake shall find it" (Matt. 10:39). For a long time our rural churches have operated in terms of a rigid institutionalization which put the church first. The result has been a church more and more lifeless, losing its life, as Jesus put it. Let us now bravely put the institutional church last and prove the positive part of our Lord's promise.

What about the minister's office? It should be clear from the foregoing discussion that he needs a room to himself where he can have the privacy essential to study. A minister's office actually serves three functions: those of study, secretarial work, and pastoral conference. Most rural ministers have their studies in the parsonages, a habit which makes the minister all too available for call by his wife for assistance in some household task or for interruption by the children. To avoid such difficulties and to assure the requisite privacy for personal conference, some men arrange for offices in the church building. But there are two difficulties to such a location: many small churches have neither adequate room for the minister nor means to heat in cold weather the room they do have; on a circuit the minister cannot handily have an office in each of his churches, and an office in any one is apt to be difficult of access for people from other churches.

A solution to these difficulties is to have an office at the trading center to which the members of the various churches go. Don Koontz, director of the LaGrange County Larger Parish, has an office in an office building in downtown La-Grange opposite the courthouse. The nearest church of the five which make up the larger parish is five miles from LaGrange, but all the people of the parish trade in LaGrange. We shall deal with the relevance of this sort of an arrangement for counseling at a later point. Here we point out that Don gains freedom from domestic interruptions by this plan. Then when he is at home he has time for the family without a nagging sense of work left undone in the parsonage office. His testimony is that for the first time in his ministry he has both a study and a home.

In most small towns such office space is readily available at a modest cost. Don pays ten dollars a month rental for his room. Ed Brewster, when serving as pastor at Richwood, Ohio, developed a plan for a common downtown office for the several ministers of the community. A suite of offices was available above the bank, and the plan involved a private office for each minister plus a common office in which they would jointly employ a secretary who would answer the phone, take care of mimeographing, mail, and appointments for all the ministers. The costs of such an enterprise divided among eight or ten churches would be individually very modest.

The advantages of such a common office for interchurch understanding and good will and a new and more powerful influence of the churches in community affairs are apparent on the surface. Sooner or later some community will find a group of ministers ready to experiment along this line.

4

The Parish Structure

WHATEVER may be our definition of the Church, this at least we can agree upon: that the local church consists of people working together in groups and as a group. Wherever groups exist over any period of time, there develop within them division of labor, systems of responsibility, and delegation of authority. These developments are essential to the growth and continuance of any group. So the early Church found it. In Acts 6 we have a picture of the dissatisfaction that arose within the Church over the manner in which the benefit payments to widows were handled. The apostles felt that they simply could not take the time and the effort necessary to administer the funds effectively. They suggested to the Church that seven deacons be elected to assume this responsibility and their suggestion was acted upon. You will recall that Stephen, the first Christian martyr, was one of the seven elected to this earliest position of church leadership.

The town and country minister will find some church structure waiting for him when he enters his parish. Depending upon the denomination in which he serves, that structure will vary. It will almost always consist, first, of a body or bodies which govern the over-all program of the church. There are often two, more or less closely related: one given responsibility for the material care of the church and the other given responsibility for the spiritual oversight of the church. Another division of responsibility between the two bodies is that between property care on the one hand and current program responsibilities on the other. These groups jointly support the church and its total program.

The minister will also find a series of auxiliary organizations more or less closely related to the church and responsible to the official church bodies in varying degrees. These auxiliary organizations include the church school, the women's society, the youth group, the choir, the men's brotherhood, young adult groups, and the like. Thus the minister of even a very small church will find himself faced with a multiplicity of groups to which he has varying responsibilities and the programs of which are not always integrated in any evident unity.

Complicated as this general situation may be, consider the plight of the average town and country pastor who serves a circuit of several churches. In his case multiplicity is multiplied. Each of his churches will present a constellation of organizations, each organization going its own intricate way. Not only is there little positive mutuality in the separate church programs, but, negatively, there may be actual animosity and conflict among churches. And this conflict is very apt to center on the preacher; he is accused of giving one church more attention than the other. Or, since his parsonage is at one of the churches, the others resent his not living in their neighborhoods and refuse to pay their share of the costs of parsonage repair and decoration. Not only is the minister involved in the programs of a myriad of organizations, but he is torn apart by the responsibility of working with organizations who work against one another. If a man is not somehow prepared for this situation, both to understand and to remedy it, it is only natural that the tension should first dismay and then discourage him so that he early seeks another parish.

When churches on a circuit are in conflict with one another, it is generally due to the fact that they are not members of the same town-country community.[1] What happens is that as long as churches are able to pay the bill, administrators subscribe to the theory that each individual church should have a pastor of its own. The unit of service is the church. Very often the village church in the trading center of the town-country community is able to pay for a pastor all its own. And perhaps so is one of the strong hamlet churches nearby.

[1] For a definition of "town-country community" see *The Church in Our Town,* Chapter II.

This leaves several neighborhood churches within the community area to be served. Often a denominational executive will add these small churches together until he makes up a salary adequate to support a minister. Churches so added are often from different community areas with no common trading habits, no common school system, no experience of working together at all. When the sole bond uniting two churches is their need to pool their meager resources in securing a pastor, then one should not be surprised if they do not work together enthusiastically or well.

If a man discovers that he is assigned or called to a circuit made up of churches from different community areas, he should realize at once that any vital co-operation among his churches is unlikely. Ultimately he should aim at such a reorganization as will relate each of his churches to churches within its own community. Meanwhile he may develop a meaningful program, but it will have to operate within the separate churches. The effort necessary to unite people in a common program across community lines is so exhausting of time and energy as to be unjustified. In such a situation a minister should seek to do the best job he can in his churches viewed as separate and distinct. The less time he spends in trying to get them to work together, the less time he will waste and the less disappointment he will court.

There are certain principles which should guide the organization of a parish and the structure of churches within the parish. We shall state them here and in each case give some suggestion as to their application to the town and country church.

1. The unit of service is the town-country community and not the individual church. Local churches are the tools for that service. This means that increasingly rural ministers should be appointed or called not to individual churches but to the service of a community area within which the several churches are the means of service. Certainly all the churches of any single denomination within a community area regardless of their size or resources should be considered as doing one

task and dealt with as a unit in securing the ministerial oversight for that task. It is this principle which lies back of such denominational terms as yoked field, pastoral unity, larger parish, and group ministry.

2. The unity of the churches within the community should find expression not simply in the calling of a minister or a ministerial staff but also in the organizing of a council. This council normally consists of four representatives from each church: the chairman of the church board, the chairman of the women's society, the superintendent of the church school, and the president of the youth group. It elects its own officers, including a treasurer who receives from the individual church treasurers their payments toward parish activities and disburses such funds under a parish budget. The members of the ministerial staff are ex officio members of the council.[2]

3. Each individual church should have a single governing body on which all the organizational interests of the church should have representation. The official board or whatever the ruling body is called should have within its personnel persons specifically designated by the several organizations of the church to represent them. Thus church school, women's society, choir, and youth group will all have their voice and vote in the authoritative organization of the church. One mark of an official organization of the church should be the privilege and responsibility of being represented on the official board.

4. The official board should itself be organized in terms of a few basic functions of the church. For example, the commission plan of organization as set forth in paragraph 219 of the 1952 Methodist *Discipline* provides for four commissions: Commission on Membership and Evangelism, Commission on Missions, Commission on Education, and Commission on Finance. Each member of the official board should be assigned to one of these functional commissions, and no member should

[2] An example of a larger parish constitution is found in the Appendix.

42

be assigned to more than one. To these commissions are delegated responsibility for all the matters that would come before the manifold committees of the ordinary church board.

5. Regular monthly meetings of the church boards and of the council should be held. In the case of many churches holding an official board meeting once a month, the commissions meet for an hour earlier in the evening; then they adjourn to reconvene as an official board to meet for another hour and to act on the recommendations, if any, from the several commissions. Thus most of the commission work and the official board meeting for a whole month can be combined in a single evening. Incidentally, in this way it is impossible for the minister to attend the meetings of all the commissions; he can remain on call during the hour they meet in case they need to consult him on particulars. It is a most healthy thing to teach laymen that they can have a committee meeting without the presence of the pastor. Many of the meetings a minister is forced to attend do not really need his help at all. Here is a way out of the heavy evening schedules we discussed in Chapter III.

There is a school of thought which rejects this suggestion and holds that the minister should attend all meetings lest the laymen "put something over on him." On this theory the minister's leadership of the group consists in getting them nominally to approve what he wants done; the thinking is program-centered not person-centered. But the Christian pastor is basically concerned not to get a program adopted but to help persons to grow into mature, responsible Christians. And this they cannot do unless we give them an experience of responsibility. To be responsible always means to run the risk of being wrong. But if God trusts men with such freedom, should not God's minister trust them too? In even the short run the minister who trusts his laymen to make important decisions on their own will find laymen who accept responsibility for living with their decisions and making successful the program they themselves have adopted.

It has perhaps occurred to the thoughtful reader to question a program which quite evidently looks toward the maintenance and perpetuation of small country churches. Such a reader might properly observe: "With your principle that the religious life of a town-country community should be unified, I agree. But why cannot that unity take the form of consolidation in a single large church in the community center? If people come to town for trade and schooling, why can they not come to town for church?" Such a question deserves careful consideration. There are several arguments which seem to substantiate the point of view that small open country churches should be maintained but integrated with one another and village churches in a single program.

1. There are religious values that thrive on intimacy—on the small group. One problem large churches constantly face is that of breaking down their membership into small, face-to-face groups in which persons can grow as Christians. A small group of people in a little church can know one another very well and live on a deep level of intimacy not otherwise possible.

2. Most small open-country churches are centers of neighborhoods. A neighborhood consists of a small number of families who visit back and forth, exchange work, and help one another in time of trouble. To have good neighbors is one of the great values of country life. In the open-country church we have an opportunity to spiritualize and make complete that mutuality and interdependence which the neighborhood provides.

3. In many cases we have closed open-country churches only to find that their members do not attend or accept the responsibility of church membership elsewhere. In many areas social differences between country and town make it awkward for country people to feel at home in the village church. If such people are to be served, they must be served by their own country churches.

4. The church should belong to the people. Not the minister's convenience or technical efficiency but the will of the

members should be the controlling force. A new practice which people accept not because they recognize it as good but because they are forced or cajoled into doing it will not achieve its end, however laudable that end may be.

For these reasons it seems best to maintain open-country churches rather than to aim at centralization and consolidation. In the long run churches which have no good reason for an independent existence will voluntarily close. Further, since the members will be the ones who decide to close the church, they will also decide to become active members somewhere else before they close their own. Thus the achievements of the old are conserved as we move into the new.

Incidentally, when churches within a town-country community are grouped together in a larger parish or group ministry, it is helpful to recognize neighborhoods as basic working units within the parish structure. One way of doing this is to break down the parish map into neighborhood sections and to mimeograph copies of each neighborhood map on regular standard size mimeograph paper. If the parish is zoned into neighborhoods for keeping track of newcomers, then each zone leader can be provided with map copies on which to keep track of his people. Persons to be sent out on the every-member canvass can receive their list of members to be visited on the back of such a map with their locations indicated on the map itself. The publicity committee can keep track of parish goings-on by the use of neighborhood divisions and can keep the maps up to date. Church and church-school attendance, circles of the women's society, and other auxiliary organizations of the church can use the neighborhood division and the neighborhood maps with profit.

From the foregoing it is evident that the choice of leadership is an important matter. Perhaps the key committee in any town and country church is the nominations committee. This committee is sometimes nominated by the current nominating committee and elected at the annual meeting along with other committees and thus tends to perpetuate itself. It should always be nominated from the floor, and its activities should remain outside the commission framework previously described.

One task of this committee should be to keep up to date a record of leadership activities of the members of the church. Harold Kirchenbauer, pastor at St. Louis, Michigan, has worked this task out in detail. Each church member has a card in the file on which are recorded offices in which he has served, attendance at board and commission meetings of which he was a member, refusals to accept nominations for office, etc. Thus the leadership record of the parish stands before them at any time. On each member's card should also be recorded any special skills and/or training he may have. A similar file of church jobs should be kept. Such jobs should be analyzed and divided into broad categories. Some are recording jobs involving the keeping of books or the filing of reports. Others are skill jobs—operating a movie projector, mimeographing, arts and crafts. Still other jobs are chiefly working with people as a chairman of meetings or committees, as a teacher of a class in the church school, as a leader of games or stunts. The danger is that we stereotype certain jobs for certain kinds of people. Older men are almost always given positions as trustees or members of the property committee. Actually what they need is to be related to other persons so that the potential loneliness of old age may be bridged. It would be more reasonable to make older men teachers in the primary department of the church school than members of the finance committee. Thus they are related to the ongoing child life in the community. With the large number of older persons present in the town and country in our day, this represents a wise and effective use of an unexpended resource.

The nominating committee should take as its principle that serving in a position of responsibility in the church is part of becoming a mature Christian. Church jobs are not to be passed out as plums nor are they to be regarded as disagreeable chores to be grudgingly accepted. Every Christian should be expected to serve his church as a part of understanding what Christian service really means. The first Christian martyr was a layman called to special service of a most unspectacular kind. In the honest exercise of his assigned task he was able to give a Christian witness that moved his enemy Saul to a changed life and that has been moving men and women to renewed lives ever since.

5

The Parish Program

THE MINISTER who comes to a town and country parish will find that a program already exists within the churches. To him it may not seem like a very relevant or effective program for a Christian church, but he will do well to remember the personal, face-to-face characteristics of rural society. What may not seem meaningful to him may have great meaning for the people whose program it is. The minister may wisely make it his rule to understand the meaning of any activity of his church before altering that activity appreciably.

An excellent beginning in program planning is to get the actual ongoing program down on paper. What is our church doing? Worship services, church school, youth society, women's work, co-operative activities with other churches, special events and celebrations—check the list and ask the officers of the various auxiliaries to help you in getting down their full program.

Then there are certain questions that almost automatically occur to anyone going over the list. Is there duplication of activity? For instance, is the women's society sponsoring a missionary speaker and is the church school doing the same just a month or so later? Might not the two organizations arrange to use the same person at the same period of time? Again, are there activities for all age groups? Is there any activity for the older women of the church? Are the high-school youth overactive? And are the out-of-school boys completely ignored by the church? Just to list the total program of the church is to begin an evaluation of it.

And that raises the question of criteria for judging an adequate town and country church program. The following criteria are suggested as offering clues to a well-rounded church program:

1. Does the program provide some emphasis on all the elements of the Christian gospel? Evangelism, Christian nurture, stewardship, missions, Christian fellowship and fun, worship, and Christian service should all find expression somewhere in the program. If any of these elements are missing or slighted, to that extent the entire program of the church is one-sided and incomplete. One way of getting a rounded emphasis is to follow the church year. As we move from Advent through Lent to Pentecost and Kingdomtide, the entire expanse of the Christian life is spread before us.

2. Does the program reflect the environment of the people? Here geography, climate, and work patterns are all-important in determining participation in a town and country church program. The time of church worship and church school will vary as between a section where dairying is the rule and an area of wheat or cotton farming. Where the work load swells to heavy proportions in the growing season, the program of the men's brotherhood will necessarily become quiescent. When work loads are light is the time for special activities on the part of the church.

3. Is the program integrated with the general life of the community? There are other churches; are they recognized as we plan what we intend to do? What of the other organizations of the community? Do we recognize the high school and its youth program and gear ours to it? Are there special days which the church ought to recognize in its program? What of Rural Life Sunday and co-operation with Grange, Farm Bureau, and Farmers Union? What of patriotic holidays and joint observances with the various veterans' organizations? From time to time church and veterans' organizations differ almost absolutely on such matters of national interest as universal military training and teachers' oath bills. It will help us to make our stand clear if the veterans find us willing to recognize them and co-operate with them in proper community patriotic celebrations.

49

4. Does the program take into account the special emphases of the denomination to which the church is related? All major denominations have programs and emphases for work in the local church which vary from year to year. These programs are often criticized as being imposed upon the rural church without its having any say or representation in their formulation and as being so planned as to be difficult of realization in a rural church. Such criticisms are for the most part well taken, and they need to be made more explicit for the benefit of church planners. On the other hand there is much to be said in favor of over-all denominational planning and general church emphases. There is a strength that comes in doing things together; a certain impetus and enthusiasm are generated when all the churches of a denomination are carrying on the same program at the same time. Then local churches are shaken out of their lethargy and challenged by outside stimulation to do things they have not thought possible. To take part in a denomination-wide program is to give local churchmen a taste of what it may mean to belong to the church universal. For these reasons denominational emphases should have a part in all our planning.

Finally, is the program as adopted and carried out arrived at co-operatively and democratically? This is really to ask: "Is this the program of the church?" We have seen many local churches carrying out the preacher's program or the plans of some small self-appointed clique; but a truly significant and Christian program always comes from the people who are the church, and belongs to them. This is true of every church, but it is particularly true of town and country churches because rural life is so personal and direct. City people are used to participating in activities with a small segment of themselves and only a nominal concern. Country people are used to bringing all of themselves to participation in all their activities. If in the planning of the church program they have not been encouraged to invest themselves, they will not be enthusiastic supporters of or workers for that program. In many rural churches the women's society or the Sunday school are almost competitors of the church services of worship. It is not unusual to have the Sunday school group leave almost in a body at the conclusion of its session and a small remnant, perhaps somewhat increased by a few new arrivals, stay on for the worship service. Undoubtedly there are many reasons for such behavior; but, among them, one we need to give account to is the feeling of lay members of the church that the Sunday school belongs to them and is their business in a way that the morning worship service does not and is not.

So much for the principles which should support our program building; now what of the concrete process of arriving at a definite year's plan? At least two months before the beginning of the church year, a request should go out to the heads of all church organizations and to the chairmen of the four commissions asking that each secure from his group suggestions as to goals and procedures for the work of the church in the following year. These are to be in the hands of the publicity committee by a specified date. It may help in the letter or notice which goes out to the various groups to list areas in which program suggestions might be made as, for example, church property improvements, additions or replacements of equipment, means of securing converts and members of the church, special educational programs, new social and recreational activities, financial askings, and leadership training. The pastor, as one of the officials of the church, will want to bring in any particular suggestions that he may have along with the others.

At the same time that this notice goes to the various officials of church groups, mention of it should be made from the pulpit in the Sunday worship service. The rank and file of the church membership are thus made aware of the opportunity all are to have to participate in planning for the year ahead, and people will begin to discuss possible undertakings with one another in the many informal contacts they make in their workaday world. Here the rural pastor has a marked advantage over his urban brother, for seldom in a city are there enough members of any single church in a work or social group to discuss the affairs of the church intimately there. But men at the lumber yard or creamery, women in their neighborhood visiting, and youth at lunch at high school, can stimulate one another in planning for their church.

When the suggestions have been gathered in, the publicity committee and the pastor should list and classify them and then mimeograph them in final form to send to every member of the church. On an evening set aside for this purpose, all members of the church are called together to consider the several suggestions, adopt goals for the year ahead, and refer ways and means of achieving these goals to the appropriate group or commission. In many denominations this meeting of the entire membership can and will be the official meeting. In others, where the governing board is more limited officially, the meeting of the members can at least refer its actions to the official body. The official agency can then take whatever appropriate action is necessary.

Someone will ask: "Is not this a relatively formal program for a country church?" That there is an element of formality in it is evident. But rural people eager to participate in the life of their church will respond to this as a practical means of getting their ideas heard and having a voice in what their church does. The Rev. Quentin Hand, formerly pastor of the Methodist Church at Culver, Indiana, and now pastor at North Charlestown, New Hampshire, has used this system for a period of years.

Once people become accustomed to this sort of planning, they may desire to set goals that reach beyond a single year's duration. A five-year plan for a church is stimulating to the performance of members and agencies. Whatever planning is done beyond the range of a single year ought to be limited to the setting of goals. If specific means are chosen for realizing a goal, these may prove irrelevant when the time comes for action, though the goal itself continues to be meaningful.

52

The following material is taken from the 1950-51 program of the Culver (Indiana) Methodist Church and illustrates the results of a planning program such as has been recommended above.

PROGRAM POLICY

The New Testament makes it clear that to be a Christian means to be in the relationship of a loving and obedient son to God as he is known in Jesus Christ.

As Christians we need at least two things. First, we need a theology to help us understand the meaning and terms of our relationship to God. Second, we need a means of being related to other members of God's family. The Church was instituted by Christ to teach the gospel (theology) and to provide fellowship for Christians with God and with one another.

Through worship, study, and service in Christ's name the Church seeks to aid its individual members to be loving and obedient children to God. Through these means the Church seeks to enrich the fellowship of each Christian with God, to enrich the fellowship of Christians with one another, and to draw others who are not yet Christians into the Christian relationship to God.

The policy of our church program is to measure each activity of our parish against the above paragraphs to determine if our activities help each member to be such a child of God and if our activities help us to fulfill our purpose as a parish church of the universal Church.

OUR GOALS, 1949-54

I. Worship
   A. An average attendance of 60 per cent of our resident members at the worship services
   B. Holy Communion on each holy day or on the Sunday following in the Christian year
   C. Observance of the Christian year
      1. In the designating of the Sundays on the bulletins
      2. By the use of altar and pulpit appointments of the proper color for the seasons of the Christian year

II. Evangelism
   A. Every nonmember of a family in which there are one or more church members, a member of the church

B. Every eligible member of the Sunday school a member of the church
C. Record some of our services and take them to shut-ins

III. *Christian Education*
A. Maintain standards of study for the pupils in our Sunday school
B. Every teacher have some training for the work of teaching
C. Offer training classes for persons to prepare themselves to teach in the Sunday school

IV. *Woman's Society of Christian Service*
A. Develop Officers' Training Day
B. Organize a circle to meet in the evenings for women who cannot attend the afternoon meetings of the W.S.C.S.
C. Hold study classes using the recommended study books

V. *Christian Service*
A. Construction of a new church building
B. An annual increase of $96 to bring our World Service giving up to $1,000 a year in the conference year 1953-54
C. Continued support of co-operative work between the denominations of the township
D. Continued support of the Scout program

OUR PROGRAM EMPHASES, 1950-51

I. To reach more persons with Christian teaching and to secure their allegiance to Jesus Christ
A. Appoint a pew host committee for each Sunday of the year to make our services friendlier and more inviting
B. Conduct a Preaching Mission in the spring of 1951

II. To open to the members of the church means by which they may give service to the church
A. Organize an Altar Committee to beautify our sanctuary through the providing of flowers and by looking after the altar and its appointments
B. Clean our present kitchen
C. Organize and operate a nursery during the worship service
D. Arrange transportation for those who are not able to attend church because of lack of transportation
F. Temporarily point up the major cracks in the foundation walls of our present building to keep water and snow from further damaging these foundations

54

III. To secure more family participation in our program
   A. Hold a Family Worship service on the third Sunday of each month
   B. Hold a Family Night program at the church on the first Sunday evening of each month
IV. To help the teaching staff of the Sunday school
   A. The Sunday School Council should recruit a Personnel Committee to secure teachers and substitute teachers when necessary
   B. We hold the following policy on teacher service. Individuals are asked to serve as teachers or workers in the church school for one church-school year. At the end of that year of service each individual will be given opportunity to continue in his position or to resign. The wishes of each individual will be respected, and those who resign will not be coaxed to continue teaching
 V. To push forward our building program in all of its aspects that we may build our new church as soon as possible

The Rev. Quentin Hand, pastor, has this evaluation to make of the procedure:

I am learning through slow and painful experience several things concerning church programs:

1. Don't try too many things at once. If you compare last year's program with this you will see that this year's is less elaborate. I have also learned to do well what is attempted. Hence, a few things well done mean more for the church than several things half done.

2. Don't try too many new things at once. Ease new items of the church program in slowly. I now try to talk new ideas over with several members of the board before suggesting them in a board meeting. Also, I begin talking about three or four months before I intend to present them.

3. Positive goals of even a five-year period mean a great deal in getting co-operation on such points as raising World Service giving, increasing attendance at worship services, and other such desirable actions.

4. Publicity is important, but more important is personal contact. The personal notes in our bulletin mean far more than the

bulletin for worship purposes. At present I am working on a zoning system for our parish in order to have more and closer contacts with the members of the church and as an aid to systematic calling.

As the various items of program are adopted by the membership meeting, it is important that assignment be made within the framework of church organization for carrying out of a specific plan. The goal of a ten per cent increase in membership is referred to the commission on membership; the women's society accepts the responsibility for the suppers in connection with the bimonthly family nights; the men's brotherhood agrees to sponsor a banquet for the high-school basketball team; and so it goes. The work of the year is seen as a whole and is reasonably shared among the workers of the church.

These plans are included for the Culver Church in a printed brochure which lists the officials of the church, contains a calendar of church events, includes a copy of the church budget itemized in detail, and provides a roll of the members of the church. Such a booklet might easily be reproduced on a duplicator by the publicity committee and provide a record of permanent interest for the church membership. Such a publication helps to make specific and practical the meaning of church membership in the local community.

Planning the Parish Budget

PERHAPS NOWHERE do pastors and lay leaders of town and country churches feel more limited and harassed than in connection with the finances of the church. In many, if not the majority, of rural churches there is an almost complete lack of system in raising and expending funds. No plan for expenditure or budget is made; no orderly solicitation of funds is carried out; when bills accumulate to a point at which creditors bring pressure, an emergency appeal is made and funds are raised to tide over the crisis. Is it any wonder that with such a lack of system there develops a conviction that there is a real lack of funds?

But this idea that town and country churches are poor and unable to pay their own way is totally erroneous. Wherever an orderly and Christian approach is made to the task of supporting the church, no difficulty is found. Some years ago I interviewed the clerk of a Pentecostal church in western Wisconsin. I knew that their pastor received no stipulated salary but simply what the people brought to him. I also knew that there were only ten families in the church which seemed a limited number to maintain a full-time pastor. Having established a friendly relationship with the church clerk, I put my problem to him frankly: "I understand you do not pay your pastor a fixed salary. I also know that his wife is in the hospital now. How can he get along?"

His reply was simple and devastating: "We believe, teach, and practice that church families should give a tithe of their income to the minister's support. There are ten families, that is ten incomes to be tithed, in our church. Since each of us gives our pastor a tenth of his income, the minister gets the average income of the families of the church. The other small expenses of our church are met by freewill offerings. Our minister should have all he needs because he gets exactly what the rest of us do."

During the war years I became familiar with the affairs of a rural Mennonite congregation. They not only maintained a full-time trained minister but gave an amount well in excess of their normal church budget to maintain civilian public service camps for conscientious objectors. The leaders of the church got the assessed valuation of the property, real and personal, of the various church families from the tax assessor's rolls of the county. They divided the total assessed valuation into the total budget needs of the church to get an assessment percentage. Then they simply sent a bill to each church family for its fair share of the costs of the church for the current year. Admittedly most churches lack such intimacy of understanding and common mind as would permit this procedure. Still the success of this Mennonite congregation in carrying a really staggering budget for four years indicates that rural churches are not necessarily poor churches.

Most of us are unhappily aware that we have insufficient funds in the treasury of the church, that we are not paying for the sort of program the church needs. But we do not know whether we would really be asking for more than our people can afford if we seek to raise the askings. Ministers realize that the largest single item in town and country church budgets is pastor's salary. To ask for a larger budget seems therefore to be tainted with selfish considerations. Set forth herewith is a plan for establishing impersonally and realistically the resources upon which the church may draw.

The Commission on Finance, or the finance committee when the church is not organized in commissions, should be called together to establish the list of families on whom the church budget must depend for its income. In some situations this list may be limited to families who have members who belong to the church; in others the list may include consti- tuent families where there is participation in the church school

58

or other activity and therefore obligation to render support.[1]

When the list is completed, a copy of it, together with a blank table like the one in Table I, is taken by the minister to the cashier or other officer of the local bank. It is explained to the official that the church is making a careful study of its financial resources and needs professional help.

TABLE I

Income Check Table

ANNUAL INCOME LEVEL	NUMBER OF FAMILIES
$ 200– 599	_____
600– 999	_____
1,000– 1,399	_____
1,400– 1,799	_____
1,800– 2,199	_____
2,200– 2,599	_____
2,600– 2,999	_____
3,000– 3,399	_____
3,400– 3,799	_____
3,800 and up	_____
TOTAL	_____

The minister indicates that he regards and keeps as confidential any information given him by parishioners, and that he understands the bank official has a like responsibility to the individuals who bank with him. He explains that he would like the official to indicate, by checking in the table, the income brackets of the families on the list; that he does not want to know the income of any individual family but rather the total income distribution of church families. It is wise for the minister to suggest that he wants a conservative figure and that in case of doubt he would appreciate an under-

[1] This matter of the constituency of the church, including the problem of building up a constituency list where none exists, is discussed in *The Church in Our Town*, pages 36 and 37.

estimate rather than the opposite; farm families should be listed as net rather than gross income.

In most cases the bank official will gladly give his help when he sees that the minister is not seeking confidential or personal information. But should he refuse to help, there are other ways of getting the same information. Sometimes the commission members can sit down for an evening around a table and make their own estimates. On other occasions a card has been sent to every family with a return, stamped envelope on which they can indicate anonymously their yearly income. By any method the minister will probably have difficulty in getting a complete coverage of all families; the important thing is to get coverage on a substantial majority.

To illustrate the procedure let us take a small town church in central Illinois with a local membership of 273 persons making up 161 families. This church had an annual budget of about $5,000 in 1951 and was served by a student pastor because its members were financially unable to secure a full-time minister. The pastor took the list of his 161 member families to the cashier of the bank and asked him to provide a table of annual incomes. For 17 families the cashier had no figures, but for the 144 others he provided the information given in Table II.

It is common statistical procedure to credit each of the families in an income level interval with the mid-point income value of that interval. Thus the number of families in a given interval is multiplied by the value of the mid-point to get the total income of those families which is given in the table in the column at the extreme right. The several interval values are then added to secure the total annual income of the families of the church. In the case of the last interval—$3,800 and up—we do not have any top limit to the amount earned. For the sake of calculation we have assumed that the limit was $4,199 and have made the mid-point value $4,000. Almost certainly this is false as there are probably incomes running up to $10,000 a year in this church. On the other hand the procedure is a conservative one, understating rather than

TABLE II

Annual Income of Church Families for 1951

INCOME LEVEL	NUMBER OF FAMILIES	MID-POINT OF INTERVAL	TOTAL INCOME
$ 200– 599	16	$ 400	$ 6,400
600– 999	7	800	5,600
1,000– 1,399	10	1,200	12,000
1,400– 1,799	10	1,600	16,000
1,800– 2,199	17	2,000	34,000
2,200– 2,599	20	2,400	48,000
2,600– 2,999	10	2,800	28,000
3,000– 3,399	18	3,200	57,600
3,400– 3,799	11	3,600	39,600
3,800 and up	25	4,000	100,000
TOTAL	144		$347,200

overstating what we have to work with. Note that with 17 families, or more than 10 per cent, unaccounted for, and with the highest income set at $4,000, the church has a total income to draw on of $347,200. The 1951 annual budget of $5,000 was less than 1½ per cent of this income.

For church members generally to give less than 1½ per cent of their income to the church can scarcely be regarded as good stewardship. Had these families tithed their income and given a tithe to the church, its income would have been over $34,000. Perhaps a tithe to the church is too much to expect, particularly as there are other benevolent causes for which we have responsibilities. Suppose we set the tithe as a norm to cover all benevolent giving; then certainly at least half of our tithe or 5 per cent of our income should be given to the church. That would mean that this particular church could expect to raise and expend a $17,000 budget.

"But," some skeptic properly asks, "isn't this a most exceptional situation? Can we take this case to be illustrative of any general rule?" The experience of the writer has been largely with Methodist town and country churches in the Middle West. In some hundreds of churches which have been carefully studied by this system, the proportion of the income in the current budget has never gone over 3 per cent. Most such rural churches have been in a position at least to double their current budgets without any sacrificial effort at all. Our town and country churches have not succeeded in making stewards of their members in any Christian sense. That fact in itself is a mark of their failure; but if we know the situation, we can with confidence remedy it.

Someone may also raise the question as to why this is given as particularly a rural church administration procedure. Of course, it would be a good tactic in any church, urban or rural. The fact remains, however, that here the rural pastor has the best of it. The intimacy of rural life means that the bank cashier will know almost everyone's income. But the situation in the urban community is substantially different. Here no single person knows everyone else's income. Some urban pastors have had success by getting figures from the local credit bureau, but these institutions ordinarily will not co-operate. A letter with a returnable card to all the membership is about the only alternate possibility; and, if the church is large, the proportion of returns is so low as to make the information thus received of questionable value.

When we have this information, how can it help us to an increase of giving? First of all it provides a realistic basis on which we can set a top figure for our budget. Knowing how much our people have to expend, we can calculate realistically how much they ought to give. Then, knowing that our askings are reasonable, we can present the budget and seek pledges in support of it with a psychological confidence so often lacking.

How shall we set up our budget? Let us return to the illustration of the central Illinois small town church, the income distribution of which we listed in Table II. Suppose we say that we shall ask our people for 5 per cent of their income for the church. That sets the outer limit of the budget around

$17,000. To raise that amount would mean to more than triple the budget in a single year, and that might not prove in an actual situation to be wise. It might be better in the long run to encourage a less radical increase. Let us, however, take the 5 per cent figure as our goal in setting up a theoretical budget and the canvass to support it.

Every church has three categories of expense for which it must plan: capital expense, current expense, and benevolences. The available funds must be spread among these three accounts. In most rural churches the capital account and benevolences suffer in favor of the current expense budget. This is at once unwise and unfair. If capital costs are neglected, then the day will come when the church is faced with the replacement of its plant because it has neglected its maintenance. If benevolences are left out, the spiritual morale of the church decays, for a vital Christian must always be concerned for and helpful to others.

The difficulty lies in appraising what proportion of the budget should fairly and safely be expended under each category. Capital costs are largely determined by the physical condition of the plant. In the case of this particular church the building is well kept and currently needs only routine care. The parsonage, however, is badly in need of a modernization program, so we ought to take some first steps in this direction. The church carries adequate fire and windstorm insurance but has no public liability insurance, that is, insurance which will pay for injuries incurred by persons using the church property. This sort of insurance is particularly important for a rural church since many old people will use the church, may easily be hurt, and often have inadequate resources for necessary treatment and care. We shall therefore add public liability insurance. The church has no debt, so no interest item need be included.

It would seem that a minimum benevolence apportionment for any church, however poor, would be a tenth of its budget; that is, we should expect at least ten per cent of the budget to go for others. A better standard would be that the church should give as much to carry the gospel to others as it expends on its own ministry. Let us set the benevolence figure equal to the minister's salary.

What shall the minister's salary be? Many other items and assessments in the budget are determined percentage-wise from this item. One is tempted to suggest that the minister receive the average salary of the church membership. In this particular case the figure would stand at $2,400. But fairness requires us to remember that the minister is a man on active duty, in most cases with a family to support, whereas many of the persons from whose incomes the average is determined are retired and not under necessity of supporting a family or of leading an active professional life. Furthermore, the minister is an educated man, often still paying the costs of his education, and is under a series of special professional expenses for books, educational refresher courses, and the like. In such circumstances it is more realistic to set the minister's salary at $3,600. That is not equal to the highest income in the church, but it is an adequate support and as such is all the Christian minister may justly expect.

Incidentally, our discussion of the minister's salary underlines the difficulty local church groups always meet in determining what that item should be. How much better off we would be if denominations put the salary of the local minister on the same basis as most of them now put their missionaries. This would involve determining a basic salary in terms of cost of living for each district or state with increments accruing beyond the basic in terms of children in the family, years of experience, and so on. Such a system would involve the payment of salaries from some central treasury with the local church paying its per capita share to that treasury. It would not prevent a local church from adding to its own pastor's stipend after it had paid its share to the general budget. It would set the salary of ministers in a dignified, just, and brotherly way.

Suggested 1952-53 Budget for X Church

CAPITAL ACCOUNTS—FOR REPAIRS AND MAINTENANCE OF OUR PROPERTY

Insurance (including public liability)	$ 300
Parsonage insulation and new heating plant	1,000
Miscellaneous repairs and upkeep	1,000
TOTAL	$2,300

CURRENT EXPENSE—FOR THE MINISTRY OF THE CHURCH

Minister's salary	$3,600
Mileage allowance (12,000 miles @ $.06 per mile)	720
Denominational assessments (pensions, supervisory costs, etc.)	1,100
Janitor's salary ($60 per month)	720
Music	600
Church school	800
Women's society	700
Youth fellowship	400
Brotherhood	200
Fuel, light, water	600
Stationery, mailing, telephone	700
TOTAL	$10,140

BENEVOLENCES—FOR OUR MINISTRY TO OTHERS

Sum equal to minister's cash salary plus $600 allowance for parsonage	4,200

CONTINGENCY FUND

	360
GRAND TOTAL	$17,000

The ordinary rural church hurts its appeal to its members and constituents by having a series of money-raising treasuries. Members know that they will be required to give not only to the church but to the church school, the women's work, and so on. Sometimes unconsciously, often consciously, they hold down their giving because they look for added appeals. The church should make a single appeal to cover all foreseeable expenses of all organizations and auxiliaries in the year ahead. Special appeals and collections should be made only for emergency causes such as flood relief. With this in mind we shall include allotments to the several societies in the budget of X Church.

These actual items and amounts are by way of illustration only, and would certainly have to be altered radically from church to church. No two churches with seventeen thousand dollars to spend ought to spend that money in exactly the same way. As we have gone along, I have tried to indicate principles by which we may arrive at a fair budgetary distribution. The above is only taken as a particular case to demonstrate how a budget may be formulated.

Raising the Parish Budget

IN THE previous chapter a method of income analysis was suggested which permits us to determine precisely the economic possibilities of a parish and to base our budget thereupon. On the basis of data from an Illinois town and country parish we set up a budget of $17,000 for the coming year. In allocating the amounts to the several items within the budget, we tried to state certain principles which will guide a church commission in determining how its local funds should be distributed. We have tried to make the budget at once realistic in terms of the capacity of the congregation to pay and Christian in terms of the order and magnitude of the several budget items.

Raising such a budget is another matter. There are all sorts of impediments to getting the money in the average town and country church. Objections are raised to making a pledge —"I do not know how much I'll earn this year, and I don't like to promise what I cannot fulfill." There are several answers which may be offered:

1. No pledge is binding if your financial situation suffers a serious reverse; we pledge as God prospers us.

2. Pledge in terms of last year's income.

3. Pledge proportionately and give the church 5 per cent of your income without stipulating any set amount.

4. You want the church to continue, and it must have some general idea of what it can count on if it is to plan ahead.

Moreover finance committees are often opposed to every-member canvasses; they assure us that such a canvass when tried in the past did not succeed. Behind this there is often a distaste on the part of the members of the committee for making such a canvass. Much of this can be changed if we educate the committee members to the real possibilities of our church membership as we build up the budget. Often by the time we are ready to talk about the canvass, they have developed their own psychological reassurance.

One pastor desired to emphasize with his people the importance of systematic stewardship as a means of supporting the church in comparison with their current dependence on hit-or-miss contributions, profits from church suppers, and the like. He challenged them to tithe their incomes with him through the forty days of Lent and to present the tithe as their Easter offering. The results were so amazing in amount secured and in the happiness of the participants that the finance committee moved the church over to a budget entirely supported by gifts in the succeeding year. The stewardship way is always the generous and happy way of supporting any Christian enterprise.

The first step in carrying out an every-member canvass is for the committee in charge to send a copy of the proposed budget to every family in the church. There is a school of thought active in many town and country churches which holds that the budget should be a secret matter known only to the inner few. Actually, the church has everything to gain by letting all its people, and indeed the community as a whole, know exactly what its costs are. Many people, for example, believe the minister is getting a much larger salary than he is. When they discover the facts, they have additional motivation to increase their own gifts to the church. The more the financial affairs of the church can be made public knowledge, the better off those affairs will be. If there is any ambiguity in a particular item, it should have special explanation in the letter which accompanies the distribution of the budget estimate. Mileage allowance might call for a special word of explanation. Benevolences should certainly be more thoroughly itemized than the simple single entry we have given in Chapter VI.

During the period associated with the setting and raising of
68

the budget, the minister may wish to preach on stewardship to give the financial appeal of the church its spiritual setting. This is undoubtedly important when a church is first starting to raise a budget substantially related to its capabilities. But once the process has begun, incidental allusions to stewardship throughout the year's preaching and teaching are sounder and psychologically more effective. Stewardship is not a special seasonal aspect of the gospel primarily associated with paying the preacher; it is the consistent and never-ending effort of a mature Christian to make what he has express what he is. Any lesser interpretation of stewardship will in the long run hurt us as Christian individuals.

The letter containing the proposed budget should go out approximately two weeks before the canvass is made. Incidentally, the names of all the members of the finance committee should appear on each letter that goes out. The week before the canvass is made, a second letter should go to each church family explaining how the suggested budget can be raised.

This explanation is best given in a table which shows the number of gifts of specified sizes necessary to raise the budget. Such a table is developed from the material in Table II. We know that we have to raise approximately 5 per cent of the income of the church, and since the low income groups have less margin, we should expect to raise a bit less than 5 per cent from them and a bit more from the upper income levels. Table II gives us data on 144 families; we have 161 in the church; we may therefore reasonably make our theoretical table for 150 families, thus rounding out our numbers. We note that there are 16 families earning less than $600. How much can we expect such families to give annually to the church? Five dollars does not seem too much. The families in the next higher category, $600–999, can certainly afford to give $10 annually; and so we go down the list. If we round off our figures to fives and tens and make the table for 150 families, we will come out with the following:

TABLE III

Gifts Necessary to Underwrite Budget of Chapter VI

15	families	giving	$	5	a year	will	produce	$	75
10	"	"		10	"	"	"		100
10	"	"		25	"	"	"		250
10	"	"		50	"	"	"		500
20	"	"		75	"	"	"		1,500
20	"	"		100	"	"	"		2,000
10	"	"		150	"	"	"		1,500
20	"	"		175	"	"	"		3,500
10	"	"		200	"	"	"		2,000
20	"	"		250	"	"	"		5,000
5	"	"		300	"	"	"		1,500

TOTAL $17,925

It will be noted that the topmost bracket of 25 families with incomes of $3,800 or more has been broken down into two gift categories to allow for the high incomes included in this category. Even then the largest gift asked of anyone is $300 a year. Thus no single family is giving as much as 2 per cent of the budget.

This table of gifts might be sent to the members of the parish in a letter something like the following:

Dear Fellow Member of the X Church:

Last week you received a proposed budget for the work of our church next year. You are wondering what your fair share of that budget should be. The Finance Committee has made a careful study of the incomes of our church members, and has arranged the following table of gifts which will produce the $17,000 we need plus a small balance to provide against losses in pledges due to deaths, illnesses, and other circumstances which prevent members from paying what they originally hoped to pay.

[here include the table]

This table reproduces the income levels of our membership. If you will place yourself in regard to your fellow members, then you can easily tell what your fair share is. If you are among those receiving the highest incomes in the community, then your gift should be $300 annually. If your income is among the lowest, then $5 a year will cover your share. Find out where you stand, pray about your responsibility, and pledge accordingly.

The budget is set at approximately 5 per cent of the annual income of our church members. In the low incomes the gift we suggest is slightly less than 5 per cent of the income; in the upper levels it is slightly more. Giving, however, is a spiritual and personal endeavor, and you must make your decision. The Finance Committee presents this table only as guidance to your Christian conscience and sense of stewardship.

Representatives of the Finance Committee will call on you next Sunday afternoon to receive your pledge. They will be ready to answer questions you may have and to feed back your suggestions into the business affairs of the church.

Sincerely,

[names of the Finance Committee]

We are now ready for the actual canvass. Many churches have a loyalty Sunday on which members are asked to bring their pledges to the church service. After the service is over, canvassers call on those who have not sent in a pledge. In a large church this serves the purpose of relieving the finance committee of a heavy burden of visiting; in such cases it is probably justified. But the average town and country church will do better by making visits to each family. This takes into account the more personal relationships of the rural community and also permits a decision to be made in the family circle with friendly visitors who can answer questions and clear up misunderstandings that otherwise hamper the financial support of the church.

The canvass ought to be completed in a single day, preferably on one Sunday afternoon. There will of course always be a few who cannot be reached and must be revisited later, but the main task ought to be out of the way by nightfall Sunday. The finance committee will have no difficulty in securing canvassers if it can assure them that Sunday is all that will be asked of them and that the committee itself will be responsible for necessary revisitation. In rural communities men should

71

make the canvass as the men control expenditures in the rural community to a very large extent, and should go in twos. If we are to visit 150 families in one afternoon, we shall need approximately 20 teams or 40 men to do the work. A single team ought not to be asked to make more than six calls in an afternoon. That permits the team members to be at ease and to visit leisurely with their fellow churchmen as they call.

The canvassers should attend church in a body on Sunday morning and be recognized at the worship service. At noon they may meet for a lunch served by the women of the church and for a brief coaching session. The budget and the table of gifts should be explained to them with plenty of time allowed for their questions. Each team should be provided with mimeographed copies of the budget and the gift table and with pledge cards. The men should be dismissed to make their calls by 1:30 at the latest.

The financial secretary of the church and the chairman of the committee should remain at the church to receive reports, and canvassers should be instructed to report back to the church with their pledges as near five in the evening as they can. Again the women should be prepared to serve coffee and doughnuts or a more cooling refreshment if the weather is warm. A large blackboard on which pledges in the various categories can be checked off as they are brought in will add interest and focus attention on the results. It is amazing how many of the canvassers first to complete their visits will remain at the church the rest of the afternoon to watch the other reports come in and be tallied. A spirit of zest and achievement develops as the totals mount. Often a team will offer spontaneously to revisit late in the afternoon or early evening in order to bring the total up to expectation.

In this connection it should be urged that every family in the church be solicited. Sometimes committee members argue that a family cannot afford to give and should therefore not be asked. The more true it is that a family should not be expected to give, the more sensitive that family will be to not

72

being asked. Every family should have opportunity to record itself, even though the record is of necessity small or negative. In cases where there seems little ability to make a pledge, the committee should send sensitive and thoughtful canvassers who will make that family feel that what is important is not the sum pledged but the spirit of co-operation shown.

Families not reached on Sunday should be called on by special teams of the finance committee as early in the week as possible. If at all possible a report of the result of the canvass should be mailed to church members no later than the Thursday following the canvass.

Suppose a team of canvassers are met, as they often are, with the question: "Well, how much do you expect me to give?" or "How much should I pledge?" The answer lies in using the table of gifts. One of the canvassers ought to say something like this: "Jimmy, we can't tell you what you ought to give. This table is prepared in terms of the income distribution of our congregation. Only you really know where you fall. Put yourself in that table where you belong." Such an answer will almost always result in the man realistically placing himself in the classification that fits him.

I have dealt at length with a conventional method of raising the town and country church budget. There are supplementary systems of financial support which are peculiarly applicable and specially devised for rural people. Two of these are the Lord's Acre and the Lord's Portion programs popularized by the Reverend Dumont Clarke, Religious Director of the Farmers Federation in Asheville, North Carolina. The Lord's Acre plan calls for the dedication of an acre of crop, a calf, a shoat, the fruit from certain trees, eggs laid on Sunday, etc., to the work of the church. A committee of the church solicits and records Lord's Acre projects at the beginning of the farming year. Crop acres or barns are marked with Lord's Acre signs and an outdoor ceremony with religious ritual is used in inaugurating the plan. At harvest time churches often have Lord's Acre auctions at which the products raised are sold to the highest bidder.

73

This system is particularly useful in dominantly agricultural rural areas for raising supplementary funds for church building and the like. Experience indicates that the Lord's Acre plan does not curtail cash giving to the church at all.

The Lord's Portion plan simply extends the idea of a member dedicating a part of his work to God for nonfarmers. Men give a day's work or the profit on the first sale on the first Monday morning of the month or some other tangible product of their personal toil. It is necessary to develop some such amplification of the plan in most churches, since people other than farmers want to participate and feel left out unless the way is opened to them. The Lord's Acre and Lord's Portion plan help to visualize graphically our interdependence with God in our work. They are excellent educational devices in bringing the truths of stewardship home to children. The 4-H Club projects often include a Lord's Acre emphasis.

Spreading the Parish News

WHILE MOST town and country churches send weekly news items to the county paper and may even on occasion insert an advertisement for some special program or event, they seldom regard publicity as a matter for consistent and systematic attention. Few rural churches have committees charged with responsibility for securing publicity for the church. The most we can expect is that an occasional church will name one of its members correspondent with the press.

Actually, almost any rural church has a more favorable publicity opportunity than even the largest urban church. The small town or county seat newspaper is always eager to give large coverage to church news. Where an urban pastor might expect a column inch on an inside page, his rural colleague can generally secure half a column on the front page. Wherever there is a small local radio station, its resources are similarly available to the rural pastor and his church. Perhaps because so much is freely ready for our use we do not make an adequate use of the opportunity.

We shall not spend time here in a discussion of kinds of newspaper publicity or how to prepare radio scripts. There are specialized treatments of these themes which the pastor should study in detail. We simply point out that the rural pastor will have far more opportunity at certain means of mass communication than his urban brother. We should be grateful for this very real advantage and make use of it skillfully.

Publicity always extends in two directions—toward the general public and toward the church membership. Often churches fail in their efforts at publicity because they do not distinguish the two audiences, or because they confuse an appeal to the one with motives appropriate to the other. The church has a solemn obligation to make an appeal to the general public, for such an appeal is the ground of evangelism. Yet often what we read in the newspaper is written solely as a news note for the faithful.

There are certain avenues of general publicity which church people overlook or the publicity value of which they do not recognize. Foremost among these avenues is the church property itself; it declares the message of the church night and day. If it is well painted, the lawn well cared for, its every feature giving evidence of loving concern, then it commends the church and religion to the passer-by. And the parsonage must be included in this publicity picture; by its maintenance people judge the church, religion, and the minister. The church is responsible for seeing that the parsonage building is in good shape and well kept up, but the pastor bears responsibility for seeing that the lawn is cut in summer and the snow promptly cleared from the walks in winter. What is better preaching of the good neighborliness of the gospel than church and parsonage walks promptly shoveled clear after each snowfall?

Many churches have bulletin boards. There is, of course, no point in having removable letters if we carry the same message on the board week after week. To do that is tantamount to saying to the passer-by: "We thought something important would happen here, and we got ready to tell the news, but nothing ever came of it." Certainly that is not the message we want our bulletin boards to carry. The location of bulletin board, as well as the message it carries, is a challenge to the imagination. There is no reason why the bulletin board should be beside the church. The Methodist Church in Bloomington, Wisconsin, for instance, is located on the hill at one side of the town; wise leadership has placed the church bulletin board with its weekly message to the general community down on the main street of the village on a lot adjoining the post office. There, where some representative of every family in town must pass at least once a day, the message of the church is proclaimed.

Here we ought to add that the church building should be clearly marked as to its denominational connection, time of services, pastor's name, and the location of the parsonage. These are common items of information that everyone knows in the average small town, but they are items which offer a real help to the occasional stranger who may be looking for the church or desperately seeking a pastor's help. If once a year a needy and troubled person can seek out the pastor and be helped because he found the church and it was clearly marked, our investment in a sign is abundantly justified.

Many rural churches possess special architectural details or equipment which have general publicity value. Sometimes a lovely spire can be lighted at night. Stained-glass windows may appropriately be illuminated from within at the high seasons of the church year. Some churches have invested in public address systems by which they can broadcast chimes or organ music to the surrounding countryside. It is important to be aware, however, that such equipment may have negative as well as positive publicity value. A church which broadcasts over its public address system too frequently or too loudly may find that it is building community ill will. Similarly spotlights or floodlights that glare in at neighbors' windows and make sleep impossible are bad publicity.

So far in our discussion we have been concerned with publicity directed chiefly toward the general public; what of the publicity which aims at the church members themselves? Let us remember here the face-to-face nature of rural contacts and relationships. Many pastors have discovered that personal interchange is an excellent means of publicizing the work of the church. Knowing the predilection of certain members of the flock for passing the word around, they make it their business to see that good news is funneled to the church fellowship through these channels. Jokes about the rural "party line" are legion; a rural pastor might well take seriously the fact that a standard means of news dissemination is the rural telephone. Why not organize within the constituency of the church a series of informants who can and will fan a message out to every member of the parish in a very short time?

As a matter of fact, the town and country pastor who organizes a publicity committee among the older women of the church is well on the road to a successful intrachurch publicity program. The women in their sixties and seventies are ideally suited for such a committee. They know the gossip channels of the community and are in a position to use them creatively. And they have time for publicity tasks. Furthermore, they feel keenly the need of something which they can do for the church. We have all heard them say: "How I wish I could work for the church the way I used to. Why when we had suppers, I'd be at the church in the morning and not home again until ten at night. But I can't stand that anymore; I just can't be on my feet that much. And I do miss it so." Publicity work is ideally suited to meet the needs of women in this category.

Most church stenciling is hastily and poorly done, often being humorous reading when it is not actually intended in that vein. The job is generally done by the pastor in snatched moments of time, or by high-school students who are both inexperienced and in a hurry. Why not turn the stenciling over to the older women of the church? Give them an instruction book, a typewriter, stencils, ink, a duplicating machine and let them figure it out. They are accustomed to following knitting instructions; they can readily teach themselves to do these stenographic tasks. In the rural community, where the higher proportion of people in the upper age brackets demands special consideration, why not use this opportunity to give older women a meaningful job to do for the church? It will lessen the pastor's physical tasks and guarantee a better quality of work than he is normally able to perform.

Such a committee of older women can organize and operate a "fan-out" system on the telephone. They can serve as correspondents with the local and church press. They can reproduce the church bulletins; edit, stencil, and mail the monthly church newsletter; prepare and send out mailings for the finance campaign, for special seasonal events, and the like. To do these tasks exercises their capabilities, gives them a meaningful relationship to the ongoing life of the community, makes them vitally useful contributors to the work of the church, and takes from the pastor's shoulders a number of routine responsibilities.

Besides general publicity and publicity directed to the church membership, there are in the rural parish certain special persons and groups to whom our message should be particularly directed from time to time. Ours is a traveling age and nation and near many small towns are motels where tourists stay. A neat printed card listing the churches of the community with their locations and the hour of their services should be available for hotel lobbies and for each cabin unit in motels. Tourists appreciate the consideration that such a card shows even when they are unable to take advantage of our hospitality. On Saturday night a Sunday bulletin made available for each motel unit is a thoughtful service.

In many rural areas we will have at certain seasons of the year an influx of resort people. It is false to suppose that these people do not want to participate in religious services when they are on vacation. We are all aware that many of them patronize the taverns more than they do the churches; but then the taverns make more of an effort to secure their patronage than do the churches. Churches can see to it that cards with the name, location, and hours of service of the several churches of the community are posted in places where resorters are commonly found: the post office, the fishing tackle store, the pavilion at the swimming beach, and so on. We should also make our buildings highly visible to visitors by signs, lighting, etc. We should stress informality of dress for many resort visitors do not bring their more conventional clothing with them.

Ours is a mobile culture, and there are newcomers entering even the most isolated communities. The ordinary town-country community will have newcomers entering its boundaries constantly, and it is the church's special responsibility to publicize its services to new inhabitants. At this point the publicity committee can keep a close watch, through its various members, of the different neighborhoods of the community and spot the new arrivals as they come. Word of their arrival should be sent to the pastor at once so that he can make an initial and official call for the church. He can and should in turn report back to the committee the age and sex makeup of the family so that invitations from various appropriate groups in the church can go to the individual members of the family. If the women's society representatives invite the wife to their meeting, if the men's brotherhood seeks out the husband with a specific invitation, if the youth group leaders seek out the high-school children, if the whole family is told about church-school opportunities, then the family cannot help feeling that religion here is an important concern and that they are wanted by the church. Newcomers are generally lonely and eager to be wanted and to belong; we as churchmen should serve them at this point.

Publicity, then, is making both the general community and our own church members aware of what the church has to offer. It is commending the gospel to all by the winsomeness and attractiveness of our attitudes and our lives. It is the daily and consistent witness which everyday Christians give to the importance of the gospel and the church in their lives. It involves the use of words but it is much deeper, when it is effective, than any words alone can be. Every church member has a part in it and a responsibility toward it. The pastor's responsibility is to make the church members aware of the influence they possess and to help them use it for their own Christian growth and the salvation of others.

Housing the Church

RURAL CHURCHES vary from one-room frame structures to beautiful and completely equipped brick and stone church plants. And not only do they vary materially, but the structural requirements for an ideal church will also vary from locale to locale in terms of such matters as climate, population density, other public buildings and resources available for the community, and the like. There is no one best type of rural church building, but there is for every situation a best church building if pastor and people will study their situation and then make the most of it.

First of all, if a church is planning to make any changes in its present structure, or to build either an addition or a new plant, it should consult from the beginning a trained architect. The Interdenominational Bureau of Architecture, 297 Fourth Avenue, New York City, is ready to give general counsel to churches making plans for new buildings. But nothing will take the place of the competent technical planning and supervision of an architect. This bureau will supply the names of nearby architects who are familiar with church problems if the church needs this information.

What will probably be of most value here is to list certain considerations of principle which should be taken into account in the planning of a church building. These principles are generally applicable, but their application will result in differing church structures as settings vary. The first principle is that a church building should be planned for the functions it is to fulfill. These are threefold. First, we raise a church to the glory of God and for his worship. That means that there must be an element of aspiration and of integrity in the structure. Ideally there will be at least one room set apart

81

for worship with its own special furnishings and equipment. Failing that in a one-room church, we can at least provide for such symbols as an altar and pulpit which can be shielded by a screen, or otherwise kept from view, when the room is used for other than worship purposes.

The second function of the church building is that of education; we are obligated to train our children in the faith and to keep learning ourselves. With regard to the actual physical requirements of teaching space, authorities in Christian education have set standards as to square feet of classroom needed per pupil of a given age. As this implies, there should be provision for separate classrooms for the various age groups. If this is impossible, then we can at least see that the furniture of the one-room church is movable enough to allow some class differentiation and separation by screens or curtains.

A third function of the church building is to provide for Christian fellowship and fun. Christians have always had a good time together: "See how they love one another," the pagan Roman and Greek world exclaimed. Even the humblest church building can manage to make room for such good times as basket dinners and socials, recreation and games, entertainments and plays. We are not suggesting these social activities as money raising events but rather as the normal expression of Christian fellowship.

A second principle in planning the church building is that the rural church should be of simple one-story construction. In urban settings, where land values are high and the supply of space is limited, there is much to be said for a multistoried building. But space is not restricted in the average rural community; to the contrary, we have acres of it. Why then indulge in a piling up of rooms one upon another when we can spread them out and thus save on construction and maintenance costs? In the second place, the rural church must serve an unusually high proportion of little children and older people. For both categories stairs represent a constant danger and, for the old people, a real deterrent to church attendance. Recently an Ohio county seat church spent over ten thousand dollars installing an elevator in the church in order that it might bring its many old people to the second floor sanctuary. If we really intend to welcome children and the aged to our services, we shall keep church buildings on one floor.

A third principle of church construction, already suggested in the foregoing, is that safety should be a prime consideration throughout. If the gospel is to save men's lives, the church which preaches the gospel should not at the same time present a physical menace to their lives. Protection from danger of fire is a case in point. Recently a new basement was dedicated in a small town church in Iowa. The windows were all closed in with glass bricks, and there was one exit only—leaving the basement by a stairway running behind the wooden partition of the church kitchen and leading not to the outdoors but to the church auditorium. A fire in the church kitchen at the time of a public supper would almost surely cut off all retreat from the building and leave the people to be burned or smothered. This principle of physical safety applies equally to the matter of sanitary conveniences. Many town and country churches will continue to use outside privies for some time to come; but these privies can at least meet the sanitary standards of the county and be kept clean.

A fourth principle in the matter of building is that the church should be planned for everyday use. Limited as the resources of rural communities are, it is difficult to justify the erection of a structure for Sunday services only. This means providing for the regular heating of the building in the winter season. Limitations of heating equipment once made the practice of heating the church only on week ends a reasonable one. Now simple thermostatic controls enable almost any church to have constant and automatic heating. In wide areas of the country natural gas is available, and this is a fuel ideally suited to automatic use. If by advancing the thermostat the church building can be ready for use, it will become much more a center of community life than it now is. Weddings and funerals now conducted in less appropriate settings will increasingly be conducted in the church. And the church building will be available for such committee and group meetings as require more space than is found in the average home. Savings in fuel effected because inefficient furnace firing is no longer needed to get the church reasonably warm on week ends will go a long way toward making up for extra fuel use during the week.

A fifth principle is that the church should be constructed in terms of reasonable future expectations. In many small villages we have today church structures capable of seating more than the present population of the village; they were built at a time when every little village expected to mushroom into a great metropolis. On the other hand we have many examples of village churches crowded into small lots with no possibility of expansion for Christian education, though such expansion is badly needed. A good rule to follow is to provide a very large lot for the church so that expansion is possible but to build in terms of a judicially conservative estimate of future needs.

Here again we must point out that the unit of service for the town and country church is the town-country community. In planning for service the population of this entire community area must be taken into account. Here is a village church with a membership of four hundred. It may need to provide for no more than that number of seats in its church auditorium. But its officers must be aware of the fact that it is the focal center for social life for half a dozen open country neighborhood churches in its community area. For this reason its social rooms may need to be built for a much larger number in order to give these fellow Christians of the community the equipment for fellowship they need.

The U. S. census provides us with decennial figures on population for minor civil divisions. From this source we can make a reasonable appraisal of the number of people to be served in our community area and also of trends in population over past decades. This appraisal, however, can scarcely take the place of a detailed, house-to-house community survey if a new church building is in prospect.

Builders ought never to forget the importance of parking space in connection with a rural church. Often the disposition is to feel that there is plenty of room to park on the road and therefore no particular parking problem. In bad weather, however, members will try to get as near the church as possible to discharge their passengers, and in practice this often means driving over the church lawn or parking on it. Besides the damage done to the lawn, this system of parking detracts immeasurably from any beauty which the church property may have for the morning worshiper. Every rural church should have a planned parking space, preferably to the rear of the church. This space should be surfaced in such a way as to provide firm parking and reasonably clear walking from the cars to the church in even the muddiest or snowiest weather. If at all possible the drive by which it is entered should pass the church entrance in such a way that old or infirm passengers may be discharged at a sheltered doorway or porch. A little thought spent in planning this out will pay dividends in human happiness and in better church attendance over the years.

A final principle has to do with the style of the building used. A church, more than any other building save possibly a home, should reflect in its lines and angles the loyalties and aspirations of the people whose church it is. It should be uniquely their offering to God, an expression of their best in a house for worship, study, and fellowship. Cornbelt pseudo-Gothic, including flying buttresses with nothing to buttress, is a symbolic expression of the irrelevance of our Christianity to our everyday life. Of course we can neither quarrel with nor condemn our fathers for building what to them symbolized a church in this new land. But now we can insist that our architects give us a building which reflects our own American feeling as to what religion is and means and does. The adobe church of the American southwest is a fine regional expression of Christianity in life.

In many rural communities where space is practically free it is paradoxically true that the children have no place at all to play. Of course they have the luxury of all outdoors to roam in, but that does not meet the need of organized sport. When other agencies do not provide play space, the church may well provide a playground with adequate equipment for the community. Such a playground might include a diamond for softball games, swings and teeter-totters for the young fry, a covered pavilion with built-in tables and benches for older folk who like to stop by for a game of checkers or chess, cement shuffleboard courts, and inevitably a horseshoe court. Such a playground requires elementary supervision. This may fittingly be provided by the older men of the men's brotherhood. They can handle the minor repairs that have to be kept up daily if equipment is to function, and see to it that the grounds are clean and that appropriate trash cans are provided and kept emptied; they can be present afternoons after school and on Saturdays to pass out such removable equipment as balls and bats. Young adult couples can take responsibility in the evening during the week and particularly on week ends for supervising the high-school crowd in their use of the several facilities. Lights are necessary for nighttime use. Thus an ordinary small town church at a very modest expenditure of funds can become a center of vital fun for a whole community.

In the long run a church building is something of which a Christian ought to be proud and in which he sees his own aspirations realized. Its lines should lift a man's spirit to thoughts of his Creator and his divine destiny, yet they should also suggest to him arms of service and love reaching out to enfold the whole world. The building and care of such a church will ennoble the men and women who engage in it. Happy that pastor who can lead his people in such an achievement.

Principles and Pattern in
Parish Worship

THE PRIMARY and unique task of the pastor is the conduct of public worship. There are many functions which he shares with other professional and lay leaders in the community: education and recreation, to name but two. But there is no one in the rural community but the pastor to assume the leadership of public worship, and this unique task requires skill and competence in its discharge no matter what other abilities and skills the pastor may possess.

In this chapter we are concerned to understand and to learn how to manipulate the worship experience of town and country people. The focus of our attention is on the problem and opportunity of the small town and open country congregation. But to understand these problems and to take advantage of these opportunities we must first think in general terms about worship, its meaning, its principles, and its pattern. Without a clear understanding of the meaning of worship our ceremonies become mere magic, no matter how much they reflect the rural setting of our congregation. Hymn singing, public prayers, anthems, baptisms, collections, and sermons are not worship; in a proper setting they are means of worship. But whether they are appropriate or significant means for a given rural situation depends not only on our knowledge of the situation but on our understanding of worship.

Worship is conscious fellowship with God. It is as rich and varied as all the activities with which we enter into fellowship with our brothers and sisters; and richer yet, since the person with whom we have to do in the case of worship is God himself.

And it is a conscious process. There is a loose sense in which every act of life is interaction with God, since to be a part of creation is to rest and to work in his will. And religion dare not lose sight of this truth lest it develop a false distinction between the sacred and the secular where no distinction is. But this continual interaction is not worship, although when it becomes the subject of our conscious attention it may lead us to worship. Worship is the conscious fellowship of human persons with the divine Person, God.

There are three principles lying behind our experience of worship which help us to understand its basic nature. First of these is the theological principle. It may be stated thus: the God whom we know in Jesus Christ has as his basic purpose self-revelation. Our God is not far off so that fellowship with him may be achieved, if at all, only after precarious journey or a scrupulous following out of an elaborate revealed formula. If the Incarnation has any meaning, it certainly means that fundamental to the nature of God is his desire to communicate his will, his purposes, and his help to men. Christian worship practices and procedures must begin with this fundamental theological postulate.

The second principle is a psychological one. It has to do with the human side of the worship experience. Human experience moves from the familiar to the unfamiliar, from the known to the unknown, from the seen to the unseen. And this is true of worship as of every other human experience. Symbols, music, ritual acts all have meaning for worship as they are familiar to the worshiper and move him beyond them to the true object of his worship. In our day there is a false aestheticism about much of our worship and a naïve faith in historic and traditional symbols and worship procedures which is perilously close to open idolatry. Many of our church buildings and much of our liturgy serve as nothing more than altars to an unknown God.

The third principle is sociological. As the theological principle dealt with the divine side of the worship experiences and the psychological with the human side, the sociological principle deals with the basic nature of the experience itself. Worship is an interpersonal, that is, a social experience. In content our fellowship with God is exactly like our fellowship with human beings, though the form of the experience is obviously different. That being the case, social experience is the background of worship. When we pray, we say, "Father." Obviously our fellowship with God is channeled and limited by our fellowship with men. And, conversely, our experience with God introduces a new quality of understanding into our relationships with our fellows. This social meaning of Christian worship accounts for the existence of a church and of public worship on a level that is strange and incomprehensible to Oriental religions.

The actual conduct of worship services involves the application of these three principles to the concrete situation in which we find ourselves. Suppose we take a somewhat typical one-room church in a rural hamlet as an example and follow through the worship process there. We begin with the conviction that God wishes to reveal himself to the farm and town folk who gather to worship him. His desire to speak to these people is not less because they worship him in a boxy wooden structure somewhat weather-beaten on the outside and smoke-begrimed on the inside. He will come to us regardless of the environment in which we seek him.

But while the physical environment offers no impediments to God, it may offer serious hindrances to the men and women who come to worship him. If the church building is poor and shabby but as good as the homes and the barns of the people themselves, then they will be able to worship sincerely therein. But if farm prosperity has brought physically fine homes and the church is still shabby, then the people who come to it will not be able to worship honestly. People who live in homes that are finer than their church are not offering to God the decent respect we offer to a fellow man; they are not being serious about their religion. We have already raised this point in connection with church finance and publicity but we must stress it here. Physically uncared for church property

89

is a fundamental impediment to worship. The church property should show signs of love and care. The lawn should be freshly mown, flower beds and bush borders weeded and clipped, the church building foursquare on its foundation. Attention to all such detail gives to the church property an air of being loved, respected, cared for, and creates in the mind and spirit of the approaching worshiper attitudes conducive to fellowship with God.

Inside the church should be clean and neat. Many a farm wife who has labored through the week to make her home clean and beautiful is prevented from worshiping on Sunday by the film of dust on pews and pulpit or the litter of Sunday-school papers accumulated in the choir loft. It is not that God withholds his presence from her. Rather her mind is so filled with the slovenly environment in which she is forced to sit to worship that contact with God is lost. As pastors we ought to cultivate the church custodian and to impress him or her with the importance of the efficient cleaning and care of the church property as necessary prerequisites for successful priestly service. When the custodian feels that he is really a fellow steward with the pastor of divine worship, then his work will improve.

The heating and ventilation of the church are important adjuncts of worship. We have previously pointed out that some automatic and thermostatically controlled type of heating can and should be secured in even a one-room church. In the first place, where the winters are severe this permits the church to be kept at a low heat all the week and assures adequate comfort for the worshipers on even the coldest Sunday. Forced firing on Saturday night and early Sunday morning may toast the air in a church that has been at near zero temperatures through the week, but it will not warm through the heavy wooden pews. Sitting on such cold pews is not only detrimental to an attitude of worship but may be a definite menace to health. Furthermore, automatically fired and controlled heating prevents that interruption of the service which comes when the custodian must add fuel or adjust drafts while worship is in progress. Even the smallest church can afford a small oil, gas, or coal heater with automatic controls.

Fresh air is always easier to heat than stale air. It should be routine on the janitor's part to open the windows and air out the building before turning up the heat. Provision ought to be made for the introduction of fresh air into the building without a current of cold air passing over necks and shoulders of those sitting near the open window. This is the only means of midwinter ventilation in all too many churches. Any church can secure a glass or composition board screen to fit tightly across the bottom of a window frame so that a direct draft of cold air does not pour onto the nearby pew holders. In cases where the heat comes from a heater through which the air is circulated by a fan, an outside connection through which the fan may circulate fresh air to be heated is ideal.

The lighting of the church presents problems for the leader of worship. If the members of the congregation, particularly the very old and the very young, are to participate in the hymns, the responsive readings, and the prayers, they must be able to see well enough to read easily. A bright stream of morning sunlight on a white page is as intolerable to the eyes as cavelike musty twilight. Indirect lighting is easier on the eyes providing it is adequately strong. The worst possible arrangement is a bulb dangling unshaded from the ceiling. When such a bulb dangles over the pastor's head in the pulpit it serves to give him a halo in the eyes of his parishioners which soon induces either a headache or sleepiness and inattention. All lighting in the choir loft and pulpit should be carefully shielded so that it does not irritate the eyes of the congregation. Pulpit reading lamps are prime offenders here. It is best to read without one if the general lighting makes that at all possible. Otherwise, be sure the light is resting below a board across the front of the pulpit which effectually prevents any light rays from going out toward the congregation. Even then the general effect of a pulpit light is unfortunate since the reflections from the white page of the Bible or hymnal

91

illuminate the pastor's countenance from a most unflattering angle.

Thus far we have spoken about those impediments to our worship of God which are presented by an uncared-for or ill cared-for house of worship. But worship in the one-room church may face other than physical impediments and handicaps. There is, for instance, the jolly and often loud visiting that goes on in the churchyard, in the vestibule, and frequently in the pews after the worshipers are seated. In the rush of conversation, perhaps keyed high to reach the less acute hearing of some aged friend or neighbor, the prelude goes unheard and the pastor has to rap on the pulpit to call the meeting to order before he can give the call to worship or announce the opening hymn. Such conversation certainly destroys the dignity and reverence with which a service of worship ought to begin.

If we remember our sociological principle, however, and take note of the social situation in which our one-room church worshipers find themselves, we shall not scold them for their irreverence or urge them to refrain from their vocal friendliness. Many of those who are here to worship have lived relatively isolated lives during the week. They have spent long hours alone in the field or woods or at household task in kitchen and farmyard, and their rush of conversation is a natural attempt to open their lives to their neighbors and friends after a week apart. If fellowship with God grows out of our acquaintance with human fellowship, then we do not under any circumstances wish to interfere with this reopening of unused paths of social interaction. Persons whose lives are reunited with human friends at the beginning of a service of worship are all the better prepared for fellowship with our divine Friend.

The problem is one of timing and of transition. The hours of the Sunday church services should be set so that all the worshipers have opportunity to arrive somewhat early. Every inducement should be extended to encourage informal visiting in advance of the service. The pastor himself may well make it a point to be present fifteen minutes early to greet the members and to set a pattern of friendliness. Even a very small church should have ushers whose main function is to assist in the transition from visiting with one another to visiting with God. These ushers should be friendly persons well known in the neighborhood and well liked. They should be counseled by the pastor frankly as to the nature of their work in connection with the worship service. When the pastor withdraws from the visiting groups and moves to the front of the church to prepare to enter the pulpit, the ushers should begin to move people from the churchyard or the back of the church to their pews. They, with the pastor, should have agreed previously upon a theme for personal devotion at the beginning of the service. Then they can say to persons as they go to their pews, "Mrs. Ed Simpson is pretty sick and they expect to operate on her in the hospital tomorrow. Let's all pray for the Simpsons at the beginning of our worship this morning." The pastor and ushers should choose their case with care, however, since if the person mentioned is not well known or if her sickness comes as a surprise to most of the congregation, the suggestion may lead to unsatisfied curiosity rather than concerned worship.

The pastor should enter the pulpit just before the prelude begins and should announce the beginning of the service of worship by some symbolic act—opening the Bible or himself bowing in prayer. If the subject of personal prayer has been well chosen and the ushers have done their part naturally, the result will be a deep silence during the prelude in which the friendliness and fellowship of the initial period of visiting will be caught up and carried over into our fellowship with God.

The subject of prayer need not be a person in physical distress. If young people are leaving for college, special personal prayer for them is appropriate. At graduation time prayer for the graduates, both rejoicing in their achievement and asking for their further guidance, is a moving beginning for a service. Gratitude for rain, appreciation of a bountiful harvest, prayer for new members entering the fellowship of the church, prayer for a couple newly married and founding their home within the neighborhood—all of these and many other topics will serve as fruitful bridges between the warmth of our renewed human fellowship and a vital fellowship with God.

Should the church afford a bulletin with a mimeographed or printed order of worship, the special theme of personal devotion should be listed at the head of the order of worship. A bulletin can be particularly helpful at this point, but it is not necessary for a church to have a bulletin to achieve a graceful transition from human to divine fellowship. Pastor and ushers working together imaginatively in a service planned to a time that does not put the people under pressure to insure prompt attendance will provide that human setting in which the divine fellowship becomes real and evident.

To clear the way of physical impediments and to utilize warm human interaction as an appropriate transition to fellowship with God are only beginning steps in our leadership of worship. We are now ready for worship itself. And here again we must have recourse to our sociological principle and remember that fellowship with God is like our fellowship with one another.

Now human fellowship follows a patterned process; this pattern is written in human nature. When we meet a friend on the street or at some social affair, our first reaction is to call him by name and to greet him. Our greeting is almost always some formalized conventional statement of our appreciation of him: we comment on how well he is looking or rehearse some recent achievement he has made or honor he has won. This leads naturally to some word of self-depreciation or apology. We have neglected to write in the interval we have been separated; we have not returned the book he so kindly lent us; with sad frequency the contact with a friend reminds us of how we have sinned against the claims of friendship; and so we put our thoughts in words. Such confession and apology—often mutual—clear the way for complete and comprehensive understanding. If there were suspicions or feelings of guilt on one side or the other, they are now cleared away and we talk freely and happily with each other or sit silently enjoying the simple fact of being together. When we are forced to part, we end our visit by some statement of commitment. Often enough it is only a simple statement, "I'll write soon," or the like, but the contact is infrequent in which there is not some sort of mutually accepted obligation at the end of the interaction.

This analysis of our meeting with a human friend is exactly analagous to our experience of worship. We begin to worship by calling God by name and by expressing gratitude and appreciation to him. This is adoration.

It is natural to move from the contemplation of God to an acknowledgment of our own weaknesses and imperfections. In the light of his greatness and goodness what we are becomes all too apparent. And our limitations seem to prevent our fellowship with God. It is at this point that our attention begins to wander or that we begin to explain to ourselves that God will certainly not listen to us. The only way out of this dryness of spirit lies in confessing our sin, bringing out into the open before God our wrong feelings and acts. This is confession and the second stage of worship.

As soon as we honestly confess our sins, a deep sense of the reality of God and his helping presence comes upon us. This sense of God's being with us leads to the third stage of worship —communion. Communion with God as with a friend may involve the most vigorous kind of thought about a problem or a responsibility; we may protest or argue, God answers, instructs, and urges us. But communion may also be simple silent enjoyment on our part of God's love.

And communion leads to commitment or dedication as we refer to this act in the analysis of worship. In the light of our communion with God, certain things appear as clearly demanded of us. Worship comes to its fruition when we accept those obligations and dedicate ourselves to doing the will of God in the specific situation involved.

95

Adoration, confession, communion, and dedication—these are the four stages of worship. Any service of worship will move naturally through them all. The occasion and the persons involved will sometimes lay stress on one element and sometimes on another, but all four are essential to a complete conscious relationship with God. And the pastor in planning his service of worship must plan for a natural development of group experience through all four. Prelude, call to worship, processional hymn, and invocation are all items of adoration. The prayer of contrition and confession, the pastoral prayer, on occasion the responsive reading, the anthem, and the scripture lesson are acts of confession. More often the scripture lesson, sometimes the anthems, often the second hymn, and generally the sermon are acts of communion. The offering, the final hymn, and the benediction are acts of dedication. It should be noted that the offering as an act of dedication properly belongs at the end of the service after the sermon, much later than it is placed in most of our Protestant church services.

Means of Grace in Parish Worship

THUS FAR we have discussed the nature of worship, the elimination of physical impediments to the worship experience, the development of a sound and natural transition from human fellowship to fellowship with God, and the pattern of the worship experience itself. There remains the question as to the means God ordinarily uses in his fellowship with men. We begin by pointing out that no list of these could hope to be complete and exhaustive simply because the richness of God's self-revelation continually transcends our human comprehension. Nevertheless there are a series of means which God has used to reach men over the ages, and to ignore these means is to improverish ourselves unnecessarily, indeed, to tempt God.

First of all God speaks to men through the Bible. It is appropriate, then, that the Bible should have a large place in our services of worship. And the Bible is a rural book. In American Protestantism we have given more and more space and time to discussions about the Bible, perhaps because of our own bias which makes the Bible unintelligible, and have devoted all too little attention to the Bible itself. In a service of worship the pastor will do well to make a relatively large use of the Bible. The tendency is to read for a scripture lesson a short selection of verses from which we have chosen the text of the sermon. We act as if a longer selection would prove boring to our congregation. As a matter of fact our failure to use the Bible at length is a confession of our own lack of discipline in learning to read the Scriptures publicly. If we study the passage in question diligently and practice reading it aloud, we shall find that fifty or sixty verses are not too much for the regular scripture lesson. We shall also find that something of the exalted style of the scripture gets into our own thinking and into the lives of our people.

But beyond the scripture lesson itself the Bible has many uses in the worship service. At whatever point we can use scriptural language and allusion in the service, we ennoble the service and enrich the experience of our people. The call to worship, the pastoral prayer, the summons to the dedication of tithes and offerings, the benediction—all offer a splendid opportunity to make use of scripture passages. It is a good rule to use other than scriptural phrases only when we can find no verse which adequately states what is required.

Incidentally, the pastor will serve his people more efficiently if he keeps a careful record of all scripture passages used in his church services. Then at the end of six months he can make a detailed inventory of his practice in this regard. A well-rounded practice would involve using passages from every section of the Bible over a six-month period. If our inspection indicates that we have not been preaching from and using certain type of Biblical literature—the apocalyptic, for example—we have our clue to begin a wider use of that material in our next services. Many of the strange and bizarre interpretations of Scriptures that gain acceptance among our people are due to the fact that the pastor has not given any attention to, or made any use of, the particular scripture so misinterpreted. Extravagant interpretations of Daniel and the Revelation are accepted because they are sown upon fallow fields. If we regularly read from and preach from all parts of the Bible, we protect our people against the exploitation of intemperate and unbalanced fanatics.

We shall have occasion to refer to preaching again, but here we ought to point out the importance of textual preaching in a rural setting. The countryman works long hours alone at routine tasks; if we provide him with a stimulating interpretation of a verse of scripture, he will have a topic to govern his meditation as he goes about his work. The miner at the coal face, the plowman on his tractor, the ranger in his lonely lookout, and the farm wife at her kitchen tasks will muse upon, mull over, and make uniquely their own such scripture as we elevate by our reading and teaching. No congregation can long fail to be Christian in which many members are opening their minds and their wills to the Word of God.

God speaks to us through great hymns. In the hymnal we have the treasury of Christian experience down through the Christian ages. The pastor who makes inadequate or limited use of the hymnal is depriving his people of a rightful heritage. This heritage to be accepted must be well known; many of our people sing and enjoy inferior religious songs simply because they have never had an opportunity to know the great hymns. Hymns should not be used in worship until they are generally known to our people; if we use unfamiliar hymns in a service of worship, we violate the psychological principle. That means that there should be some regular opportunity for our people to learn unfamiliar hymns in preparation for their use in worship. A midweek service is an excellent opportunity to have a hymn sing in which new hymns are taught. To teach hymns successfully the pastor should have a hymnody in which the various tunes are discussed in terms of their authors, their origins, and their histories in the life of the church. Often the choir can help make a new hymn familiar by using it as an anthem.

In this connection we are often faced with a problem regarding the piano or organ accompaniment of hymns in a rural church. The pianist is a person of relatively little skill who can play a few of the hymns when called upon to do so. The answer lies not in permitting the pianist's meager repertoire to limit use of hymns but in giving the pianist a chance to learn the hymns in advance of the congregation. It is a courtesy to supply your choice of hymns for the service to the pianist a week ahead of their actual use. That gives her an opportunity to practice those with which she is not familiar in order to be ready to play them with decency and dispatch in the actual service of worship. It will also give her a happy feeling of confidence and growth which will

99

enable her to play with vigor and assurance, and thus prevent that hideous dragging of the measure which lends so soporific a mood to rural worship.

God speaks to us through public prayer. There is no more noble English usage than that found in the *Book of Common Prayer*. Every pastor should have a copy of it, not in order to use the prayers in his own free worship necessarily but to develop by frequent reading of those prayers a lofty use of English in his own spontaneous public prayers. In churches not accustomed to a fixed liturgy there is often a tendency to be critical of the formalism and the repetitiousness of a liturgy. As a matter of fact so-called free prayer can and often does become more fixed and formal than the most stilted liturgical service. When the pastor arises to lead in prayer, we know exactly what he will say, the course his thought will take, the allusions and metaphors he will use, and even the time he will take with the performance. In addition his language will lack the beauty and comprehensiveness of the great written prayers. Such free prayer constricts God's free revelation more than any fixed liturgy could do.

Truly free prayer is not unpremeditated or unplanned. It is more accurately public prayer based on the theory that after full preparation has been made there is something in the public service of worship in which a pastor and his people turn together toward God which enables the pastor to frame their common petitions more effectively and comprehensively than he could if he depended entirely upon a previously written prayer.

In what does a proper preparation for such prayer consist? First, we must remember that public prayer is prayer on behalf of a congregation. To that end we ought to meditate upon the needs and interest of our people. I have found it helpful to go over the roll of the parish membership name by name thinking of the situations, problems, and joys of the various individuals and families as their names come up, and jotting down notes as to effective subjects for common prayer. A second source of help is thought about the season of the year

100

and appropriate petitions in connection with it. In a farming community rain or the need of rain are certainly subjects for prayer, as are also bountiful harvests, safe recovery from the danger of flood or cyclone, the beauty of the spring landscape, and the joy of hard outdoor work. Third, there are the events both local and world-wide which have a Christian repercussion; these should be in our praying. Fourth, there is the will of God for our lives; we ask the question: "What does God want us as pastor and people to do?"

With these four factors in mind the minister may outline a prayer following the general outline of worship we have already discussed: adoration, confession, communion, and dedication. His outline is possibly detailed as to actual phrases by which God is to be addressed or in which a particular petition is to be made. Then on entering the pulpit to conduct the service he may discard the outline knowing that its preparation has now become a part of him and will become the vehicle through which the Holy Spirit of God will lead our common prayer when we together turn to him. Such an outline does not handicap or stultify the freedom of inspired prayer, but it does guarantee that the minister shall offer to God a preparation and a discipline at least as serious and wholehearted as the task in which he is engaged when he leads his people in prayer.

In relation to the subject of prayer it is appropriate to mention the use of poetry in the worship service. Occasionally in his prayer, or elsewhere in the service, the pastor will quote from some poetic source. Now literary taste is not an inherent but a cultivated thing, and poetry is not good because it rhymes or expresses morally commendable sentiments. All too often the type of verse quoted by the pastor offends the good taste of those in his congregation who understand and love poetry, while it does nothing to lift and ennoble the taste of the others. The only safe rule is to depend upon the great anthologies of poetry exclusively for his selections until, from wide acquaintance with their contents, he has developed high

101

standards of poetry in himself. Anthologies which will prove helpful are included in the bibliography.

The pastor, in his use of poetry, must also take into account the literary tastes of his congregation. Many rural persons have a relatively limited knowledge of poetic literature. Their common attitude is that poetry is difficult to understand and trivial. In all probability their judgment is a correct one on the basis of the verse they have known. The pastor who chooses carefully from among modern poets—Robert Frost and Robert Francis, to name but two—who have loved and made memorable town and country experiences will bring to his people a revelation of joy and beauty not only in the poetry but in their own rural experiences as well.

God speaks to us through silence. I do not mean through periods of soft organ or piano music, although their use in worship has its place. I mean silence: the complete quiet of all instruments and voices before God. Our usual error in attempting to use silence in a service of worship is to introduce a period of silence without adequate preparation for it either in the prior parts of the service or in the experience of our people. Silence should not, except after long familiarity, be used at the beginning of the service. Rather it should be a part of the service toward which we build so that the silence when it comes will not be a mere cessation of noise but a true opening of the individual to the spirit of God. Silence just after the reading of the morning scripture lesson before the pastoral prayer is a most helpful experience as is the silence that precedes the benediction. But wherever we use silence it should be the goal of a preceding process of worship and not an isolated period in which nothing is being said, sung, or done.

The worship symbols of the church building may also be a means whereby God speaks to his people. We have already mentioned the semi-idolatry that goes with an unthinking veneration of traditional Christian symbols. Unless a symbol has meaning for the people who use the building, it may have aesthetic excellence and historic authority but it does not serve to open the way for men to God. There is a whole series of Christian symbols, growing out of the rural life in which the writers of the Bible lived, which are most suggestive for the rural sanctuary. Among them are the shepherd's crook, the vine and the branches, the sheaf of wheat, the lamb and the shepherd. Among the most meaningful symbols is that of the yoke. Some rural church will one day place a yoke over the door by which the congregation leaves the sanctuary with the inscription below it: "Take my yoke upon you."

In addition to traditional symbols, objects having symbolic value for the particular church will often be found. An old communion set given a place of honor, the remnants of the cornerstone of the earlier church building, the shovel with which ground was broken for the new church, all have particular meaning in directing the mind of the worshipers to God. Through such special symbols God often speaks. No symbol is too mundane or homely to have its place of honor in the church if it carries a freight of precious and reverent memory to the people who worship there.

God speaks to us through nature. For the countryman nature is his most immediate and familiar environment. Its power, its lawfulness, its resurrection in growth, its beauty, its changeableness with the seasons—all of these characteristics of nature and more he notes and muses upon. The town and country pastor who makes reference to natural phenomena in prayer or sermon must take special pains to be sure his statement is correct, for he speaks to people who know of such matters from long personal experience. More often than not we can use the insights and observations of the more discerning among our people as the basis for our own appreciation of the divine revelation in nature.

Finally, God speaks to us through the sermon. This is not a book on preaching, and hence we cannot do justice to the sermon here. We do wish to speak out, however, against that view of preaching which contrasts worship on the one hand with preaching on the other. Such a view has no place in the evangelical churches for preaching with them is never simply instruction. Among evangelicals the function of the sermon is not only to describe Christian experience and to commend it to the hearers but actually to reproduce it at the moment of preaching. And as such the sermon is not an afterthought to worship but the goal and climax of worship itself. If the Word is to be made flesh, it nowhere becomes flesh more explicitly than when the pastor, who knows and loves his people and who has studied and listened to know God's will for them and himself, stands before the congregation to declare the Word of the Lord.

12

Sacraments in Church Worship

CEREMONIAL celebrations of life's great events are
among the priceless heritages of Christendom. In Baptism we
declare God's concern and our own for birth and growth; in
the Holy Communion we celebrate the redemptive power of
fellowship and of self-giving love; in the wedding we mark
the culmination of love in the founding of a home; in the
funeral we assert man's immortal hope on the occasion of his
ultimate defeat. That these rites mean much more than the
celebration we have indicated, we would of course agree. But
that they do have these vital meanings, we would insist.

And nowhere do these ceremonial celebrations have more
warm human significance than in a town and country parish.
In urban life with its segmentalisms these rites tend to be
familial or, at most, special group concerns. Among rural
people they are community concerns, matters of public celebration, occasions for common participation in a way that they
seldom are in urban life. Young men beginning a rural pastorate are often astonished by the closing of stores in a small
village and the crowding of the sanctuary for the funeral of
a relatively undistinguished citizen. In a society where people
are limited in numbers and deeply dependent on one another,
the loss of a single citizen by death is a serious challenge felt
by all and acknowledged by general attendance at the final
rites on his behalf. In the death of this person every individual
has suffered a personal loss, a loss which he thinks proper to
recognize in a religious ceremonial. The rural pastor must
always remember that as he conducts the various ceremonial
rites he is acting in a representative way for the community as
well as for his parish.

We ought also to observe that there are extremely limited

opportunities in the rural community for publicly sanctioned emotional expression. Occasions of public pageantry, parades, theater events, concerts, even the thrill of participation in the vast crowd of persons assembled in the stadium for a football game are quite generally lacking. But people everywhere need the emotional outlet that comes from conventional crowd participation and the lifting out of themselves made possible by theater, opera, and symphony. The revival is one such reaching out for a community sanctioned emotional expression on the part of rural persons. Town and country pastors should appreciate this basic need of their people and conduct the high services of rite and sacrament in a way which will develop the emotional elements inherent in these occasions.

Let us consider the baptismal service. To begin with we need to remember that baptismal practices differ among Christian groups and that what is said here must be adapted to the polity of the particular denomination in which the pastor serves. The only element common among Christian fellowships which baptize is the baptismal formula: "John Oliver (using the person's given names), I baptize thee in the name of the Father, and of the Son, and of the Holy Spirit. Amen." Young pastors should be careful to use this form exactly, not because the words as such have any magical value but because they are one of the few common possessions which these fellowships share and agree upon as Christian.

Let us begin by dealing with the baptismal service for infants and then later consider the practice of adult baptism. Incidentally, most of what is said here will apply to the practice of dedicating children to God which is increasingly finding acceptance among Christian fellowships who reject infant baptism.

Suppose the Tom Putmans are having their first-born son baptized on Sunday morning. To begin with, we notice that the attendance at the service is larger than usual; families who are not members of the parish are awkwardly present. This augmentation of the ordinary congregation whenever babies are to be baptized should lead the pastor to avoid in

106

his sermon any merely parochial theme and to preach with the expectation of sharing Christian truth with a high proportion of Christian illiterates. It should mean that ushers are alert to mark the new attendants and to give them such personal greeting and guidance as will help them to feel less awkwardly conspicuous and more at home.

What a freight little Eddie Putman carries as his parents bring him forward to the altar rail of the church! Most members of the congregation know his grandparents and his parents, his uncles, aunts, and cousins. Even his name, Edward, he shares with the great-grandfather now deceased who came to these parts and took up a homestead in the pioneer days. They remember how Tom courted Anna Griswold; how the two young people began to go steady when Tom was star forward on the high-school basketball team. Most of the congregation were present on the June day when Anna walked down the aisle of this same little church to meet Tom at the altar. Everyone knows how Tom and Anna wanted a baby; how they lost their first child and almost lost Anna's life, too, in a miscarriage brought on when their car skidded into a ditch in the winter blizzard two years ago. When Tom and Anna walk forward, Eddie held proudly if stiffly in Tom's arms, there is a sense of community triumph. The life of the town, the cherished values, are all caught up and proudly displayed in a three-week-old baby in his father's arms. The words of the service, the water with which the pastor touches the baby's head, the baptismal formula are all the same in an urban or rural service. But obviously what the pastor is doing in the rural service is of more comprehensive significance than the same service in an urban setting. Here are caught up and celebrated not just the joy of parents and their friends at the birth of a son but the joy of a community in the ideals and achievements of a family over the years. The pastor as he conducts the baptismal service of Eddie Putnam is helping even basically unreligious people to say "Amen" to a certain quality and integrity of life.

107

In such a service there should be no room for the sentimental or exhibitive. Such extrinsic elaborations of the service as the use of a flower to baptize the child or the kissing of the child by the minister are totally out of order. God has given us this child just as he has given us over the years so many other good gifts, and we dedicate the child to God's way—just as we ourselves are dedicated to that way—assured that God will prosper him in it. Anything which draws attention away from this all-important transaction is essentially sacrilegious.

Evangelical churches by and large do not follow the practice of having godparents at the baptism, but there are many rural situations in which this custom is maintained. In this case the godparents bring the baby to the chancel and take the vows which the parents otherwise take. Our evangelical practice permits this but insists that the parents themselves take the vows as well. It is a holy practice for a couple other than the parents to feel and assume responsibility for the child's Christian growth.

Whatever the form of baptism we may use, we should strive in the service to indicate God's concern and purpose to surround the individual with redemptive love at every level of his life. On occasion we shall be asked to immerse persons at their baptism. The appropriate place for baptism by immersion is some stream or lake. The pastor should make sure of the bottom of the stream before he conducts the service lest stepping into a mudhole or a sharp step-off in the stream might lead to a comic rather than a dignified spectacle. The principals should wear bathing attire under simple cotton clothing and should be instructed carefully as to exactly what they are to do. An open-air immersion can be a stirring service if it is conducted with order and preparation. Congregational singing led by the choir during the service makes a most beautiful background.

Protestants generally recognize two sacraments: Baptism and the Lord's Supper. What we have already said in connection with the first regarding the proper solemnity and dignity with which the service should be conducted applies with the same cogency to the second. It is also true of the Communion service that customs regarding its administration differ from denomination to denomination. The part that laymen play in the administration of the sacrament, the manner in which the elements are served and received, as well as the form of the ritual, all vary in details among the churches. The pastor must adapt whatever suggestions are made here to the polity of his particular fellowship.

The Holy Communion was inaugurated when a little company of countrymen joined their leader at the table for a ceremonial meal. The intimacy of the rural church congregation offers unusual opportunity to make the sacrament meaningful, but it does not guarantee this meaningfulness. Intimacy may result in carelessness as was the case in the Indiana parish in which the pastor found his Communion steward using grape pop as the sacramental liquid. Intimacy also leads to a knowledge of one another's weakness, and we may be repelled at taking communion again and again with one who promises to live "in love and charity with your neighbors" and goes back to the same old sins each Monday morning. It may help us in such cases to remember that among the twelve at the first memorial meal were betraying Judas, denying Peter, and the other disciples with their worldly ambitions and rivalries, their misunderstandings and disloyalties, their doubts and fears.

There are often in the rural parish unique aids to a meaningful observation of the Lord's Supper. Sometimes the Communion steward is a farm wife who prepares the sacramental liquid from her own grapes and herself bakes the bread from which the wafers are broken. When the elements the congregation receives are the product of loving hands and the personal labor of one of their own fellowship, the ties that unite us to one another and to God's world around us are made more clear and emotionally compelling. All the homeliness of a memorial meal among dear friends is possible in the rural Communion service.

We have earlier mentioned the importance of the congregation using the hymnal of its denomination rather than some songbook. We return to the matter because the hymnal always contains the ritual of the Lord's Supper. If people are to participate meaningfully in the sacrament, they must be able to follow the service with familiarity; such familiarity may be readily achieved if they have available the service in the hymnal they customarily use. Such guides and help to worship make the hymnal more than a mere songbook. It is actually a major aid in worship.

The observance of our Lord's Supper unfortunately often becomes the occasion for disturbing experiences in town and country churches. Where custom dictates that communicants come forward and receive the elements at the chancel rail, they are often compelled to look at undusted expanses of floor which are not ordinarily within the view of the worshiper. The pastor ought to accept as one of his responsibilities in connection with the service the task of kneeling as the worshipers will at the chancel rail to observe whether their view will include the results of careless housekeeping. Again he should check to see that the chancel rail itself is free of protruding nails or splinters which might produce injury to communicants.

In churches in which the choir is seated across the front of the sanctuary, the communicant is often faced as he kneels at the altar with a miscellaneous collection of feet and knees belonging to the choir members. In addition he may be conscious that the choir members are looking down at him as he communes and are thus intruding at a sacred moment. If the choir is located thus unfortunately, the pastor can obviate the difficulty by asking the members to commune first and then to take seats in the front pews during the remainder of the service.

Another cause of disturbance lies with the occasional visitor who attends church on the morning Holy Communion is to be served. He may be unfamiliar with the practice of the church he is attending and not aware of limitations it may set to participation in the service. The pastor has a responsibility to make clear before the administration of the sacrament

110

the terms under which the service takes place. If closed communion is practiced, then that should be made clear and an opportunity given for non-communicants to leave the church before the administration of the sacrament takes place. When open communion is practiced, that should also be clearly stated. My own custom has been to make the following statement before the administration of the elements in the interest of resolving any confusion in the minds of worshipers: "Our church regards this table not as our table or the table of the Methodist Church but as the Lord's table, and we welcome to it any who are welcomed by him. Our custom is to receive the elements kneeling at the chancel rail; but if by virtue of conviction or infirmity you prefer to receive them standing or seated, come forward and stand at the altar rail or be seated in the front pew, and you will be served. Our sole requirement is that you receive the sacrament with ungloved hand."

In most rural churches there are several older persons who find it difficult if not impossible to kneel to receive Communion. Such a public statement by the pastor as the one above will make it seem natural to them to receive the elements standing. Where our church practice is to come forward and kneel at the altar for Communion, we ought to be particularly conscientious as pastors in seeing to it that infirm persons are made welcome at our administration of the Lord's Supper. If one or two on our personal invitation prior to the service come forward and receive the sacrament standing or seated, others who suffer a similar handicap will quickly develop the practice and thus be enabled once more to participate in the full sacramental life of the church.

13

Rites in Church Worship

THERE IS a whole series of rites in which the pastor leads his congregation from time to time. These vary with the denomination and the locality in which he serves. Two, however, he will administer everywhere and constantly: the wedding and the funeral. To these we will devote our attention in this chapter. To ignore the reception of members or other dedicatory rites and services is in no way to reflect upon their importance. Rather the variation in practice among the several evangelical churches makes any general treatment impossible.

In the wedding a man and woman bring their high human commitment to each other and ratify it for all time in a commitment before and to God. Unfortunately the wedding is often marred by horseplay and practical joking which may be regarded as humorous in the particular rural locality. There is something to be said for good fun and fellowship on such an occasion, though the kidnapping of one or the other of the wedding principals hardly falls in this category. The pastor as a member of the community entering into the good times can and should exert a moderating influence upon them. He can control the horseplay so far as the wedding itself is concerned by educating his people to the conviction that the church is the only appropriate place in which to be married. He should also lodge with his official board the responsibility of setting up concrete standards and limitations as to the use of the church building. These regulations should deal with such matters as the decoration of the church, the use of the church property for a reception, and the limitation on photographs before, during, and after the service.

On occasion church auxiliaries have given mock weddings

as a means of entertainment. To do so is about as appropriate as to burlesque a baptismal service. We may be able to convince our people of this fact only gradually; but certainly we as ministers stand within our rights when we refuse to have any part in such a mockery. Should a minister be asked to take part, it is proper for him to say, "I simply cannot do it. Would you like to remember me presiding at a mock wedding when you look up to the altar as I conduct your daughter's wedding?"

In marrying a couple the minister always acts in a dual capacity, representing not only the church but the state. This involves him in certain legal requirements. He must be certain of his own legal right to perform a marriage. Requirements differ from state to state. Some states insist that a clergyman be a resident of the state before he performs marriages; others, that he register with the county or village clerk a copy of his church credentials. A minister as soon as he moves to a new community should ascertain the regulations governing marriages and fulfill whatever requirements there are.

A minister should also determine whether a couple coming to be married is legally qualified to marry. This involves not only their having a marriage license but one valid within the community which the minister serves. The minister, of course, is not responsible if in ignorance he honors a marriage license which misrepresents the status of the principals; but if he knows them well enough to know that the information there given is incorrect and the license accordingly invalid, he cannot lawfully perform their marriage and is held responsible for maladministration if he does. It is the minister's special duty to know the laws of the jurisdiction in which he serves and to administer them rigorously. We certainly do a couple no favor in marrying them under circumstances which later may call in question the validity of their marriage and the legitimacy of their children.

As representative of the church the minister must also enforce its canons regarding marriage. Denominations vary as to the rigidity with which they interpret and enforce the Biblical injunction against divorce. Some refuse categorically to marry a divorced person whose former mate is living. Each pastor must determine what the rules of his own fellowship are and then enforce those rules as honestly as he can. He may not always find himself in agreement with them, in which case he has an honest obligation to work for their change; but he is also obligated to enforce the existing rules scrupulously whatever his own opinion may be, since he is serving as representative of the church when he performs a marriage.

The wedding is surrounded with social customs of which the minister must often become the interpreter in the rural community. Such customs are simply customs and may be varied to fit the need and mood of the particular occasion. The minister should be ready in the case of a formal wedding to direct the entire matter at rehearsal and to instruct the family members in good form if they have any question as to how the proceedings should go. References to appropriate books on wedding etiquette are given in the bibliography.

In the midst of all the emphasis on the form of the service the minister dare not forget or allow the participants to forget the ultimate nature of the service itself. After a wedding rehearsal I have found it helpful to say to the prospective bride and groom something like this, "We have gone through the service step by step in order that you may be familiar with what is going on during the ceremony. Now I want you to forget everything that we have said and done together. My business is marrying people, and I'll see that you go through the service. What I want you to think about is your love for each other and the fact that you are committing your lives to each other before the presence of God. Remember that and I'll see that you do and say the right thing in the service." Under such counsel I find that the couple come to the service relaxed and able to participate in it with freedom and joy rather than tense because they are trying desperately to remember what they are to say or to do next. Such a word helps to lift the wedding service to its true horizon.

While all rites and ceremonials have their peculiar color and significance in relation to the town and country church, it is in the conduct of the funeral that the town and country pastor will be most likely to find himself facing characteristic problems of rural society. Rural familism, for example, dictates that members of the family attend the funeral of even a distant relative; hence we have the delay of the service while persons at a distance are on their way, the problem of entertaining such visitors in a community without public accommodations for transients, the fact that each funeral tends to become a public occasion with business at a standstill and the church crowded with those who come from a sense of duty as well as those present from a sense of grief. The rule of custom may further provide that an obituary be read at the funeral service. The pastor entering a new charge had better be prepared for this or he may be handed a lengthy obituary to read as he is starting into the pulpit with his service carefully planned, and find himself stumbling through a mouth-filling list of strange names or hesitating over several stanzas of hopelessly sentimental and shoddy verse.

The funeral service is ideally held in the church, whether the deceased was a church member or not. The man whom God has taken is clearly welcome to a final service in the house of God. Funeral services in homes suffer from overcrowding, from the lack of any fixed physical orientation to bring unity to the worshipers, and from the familiar associations of home life. Services in undertaking parlors or funeral homes may be held under more commodious and comfortable circumstances, but the atmosphere of secularism and commercialism so frequently evident is a serious handicap. Every minister will find himself at times conducting services in homes or funeral parlors. The time of death is not the occasion for insisting on practices to which people are unused; but before the shock of bereavement comes, we should be educating our people to the conviction that the church sanctuary is the proper place for the funeral service.

A series of impediments to worship arise in the social situation and the psychological atmosphere of rural funerals. To begin with, the congregation is almost always a heterogeneous one with persons of Roman Catholic as well as Protestant faith, or with no religious tutelage at all, striving to worship together before God. We cannot count on the common understanding and response that we depend upon in our Sunday worship fellowship. Furthermore, commercialization and secularization are hindrances: the corpse is made to look more lifelike than the living, flowers are overwhelmingly profuse, the elaborate casket speaks of anxious striving to meet the demands of social prestige; above all, there is the atmosphere of capitalization upon the mourners in their time of deepest need and loneliness.

The emotional condition of the mourners themselves is another impediment to worship. In rural areas where hospitals are scarce, members of the family are often physically exhausted from long days and nights of care of the deceased at home. Many times this physical weariness is deepened by a profound sense of failure. Time, money, energy, and prayer have been expended, and the forces of death have proved stronger than any available resources. Sometimes there is in addition a sense of guilt which carries particular weight in the rural familial setting. The daughter who lives at some distance quarreled with her mother when they were last together, and the two parted with harsh words. Now the mother is dead, and the words have a final quality that was never intended. There can be no asking of pardon now, no human reconciliation. The impossibility of making things right with her mother becomes a barrier between the daughter and God.

In addition to such specific emotional factors there is the universal pain of bereavement itself. From the family circle a person upon whom others depended and to whom they looked for specific satisfactions is taken. Needs he or she formerly met must now go unsatisfied or find satisfaction elsewhere.

116

Such readjustment always makes for emotional confusion and inner conflict. Persons thus turned in upon themselves are not easily directed toward the outward reach of worship. Emotionally they are handicapped for turning toward God.

To refer to these impediments is simply to remind ourselves of the extra planning and thoughtful care necessary if the funeral service is to be worshipful for those most intimately involved. In our arrangement of the service such factors must constantly be in mind. Simplicity of presentation, unity of approach, repetition of a single theme, the use of familiar Biblical passages, strong rather than sentimental music and hymns—these should always characterize a funeral service. Aware of the specific impediments in the situation, we shall be able to react intelligently to them and thus to guide our people into a worship of God in spite of those elements which stand in the way.

In the section dealing with pastoral work we shall have more to say about calling on the dying and on the bereaved. Here we need only to emphasize the fact that the pastor ought to call regularly and frequently on all his people and with particular promptness and fidelity when any member is reported ill. We are distinctly under handicap when we are called to conduct a funeral for a family with which we have not previously been familiar. The fact that we have failed to call, however, should not keep us from going at once to visit the family when a death is reported to us. A prompt call on the bereaved cannot atone for previous carelessness or neglect, but any delay at this point is completely inexcusable.

There are four items of information which the pastor must secure from the family in planning a funeral service: (1) the time of the funeral service; (2) the place of the funeral service; (3) the place of the interment; and (4) any requests the family may have, such as scripture to be read, music to be played or sung, and personal allusions to be made by the pastor in his sermon. Not all of this information needs to be gathered at the first call however. We call first as pastors and may well dismiss everything from our minds except our spiritual minis-

117

try to persons overwhelmed by grief. Obviously the only fact that needs to be ascertained at once is the time of the funeral service. This should be set in order that relatives at a distance may be notified, announcements may go to the press, the church building may be reserved, and the responsible public servants participating in the ministry of the funeral instructed. The pastor is the one who has the final word to say as to the time of the service. We should not permit the time of funeral to be set without our consultation. This does not mean any arbitrariness on our part. It does mean that the pastor must have the final word, because otherwise there can be no check on conflicts in funeral dates. If we do not insist upon this matter, we shall sooner or later be faced with the tragic dilemma of two funerals set by two different undertakers for the same hour of the same day. Both families will be counting on our services, and there is no easy way out of that situation. Ordinarily we simply inquire of the family and the undertaker as to the hour they prefer and then, if that is at all possible to us, we indicate our acceptance. It is a matter of courtesy on our part never finally to set the time of a funeral service without consultation with the undertaker, should he be absent when we interview the family.

At the close of the first call on the bereaved the minister may easily ask if it is convenient for the family to see him at a certain time the next day. At this time the entire pattern of the service as far as that involves the family members may be worked out. Often we find a large group of neighbors and friends present when we come to interview the family the second time. It is never discourteous, after we have greeted all those present and visited generally for a minute or so, to ask to see the immediate family alone in another room to perfect the funeral plans.

Items two and three in the foregoing list are self-explanatory. The fourth item needs some exposition. The pastor always wishes to give his people an opportunity to express their wishes with regard to the service. But he should always frame his questions in such a fashion that the bereaved will not feel

118

compelled to offer suggestions when they really have none. He might say something like this: "I have known your mother over the years, and I have some ideas as to the proper sort of service for her funeral. However, I want to make it a service in which we will all participate to the full. Therefore if you have any scripture you would like to have read as your mother's favorite or yours, I'd be glad to know about it." We can deal similarly with the matters of music and sermon.

Most of us feel acutely the problem of music at the funeral service. We have seen how a sentimental song sung at the close of the reading of the scripture can nullify and dissipate the ministry of the Word. Perhaps the best music for a funeral service is organ or piano playing and congregational singing of great hymns. In the average small town or open country church, if there is to be vocal music, it is safest for the minister to make the arrangements with the soloist or choristers. Then he will be able to interpret something of his purpose and plan in the service to them.

In this connection we ought to be aware that it is often not the quality of the music but the person of the musician which makes the chief contribution to the funeral worship. In one rural community an older man was asked to sing at many funerals; his voice had never been an unusual one, and the years had placed their limits upon it as well. Nevertheless he was asked to sing again and again, because his personal integrity in the community made his singing at a funeral a kind of community benediction on the life of the deceased. The value of such a service cannot be evaluated in terms of musical excellence alone.

An appropriate order of worship for a funeral is:

> Prelude
> Call to Worship
> Invocation
> Solo or Anthem (if requested)
> Reading from Old Testament
> Reading from New Testament
> Solo or Anthem (if requested)

Pastoral prayer
Sermon
Prayer and Benediction

The word "sermon" is used here in place of the nondescript term "remarks" to indicate that the only proper address at a funeral service is homiletical. When we stand before God we do not memorialize the dead, we declare his Word for the current crisis. Granted that this Word may be one of comfort and assurance and hope; we are still preaching, and no other form of address is appropriate. There need be no sermon at a funeral, and whatever sermon is preached should be extremely brief.

In the funeral service the minister is co-worker with the undertaker or funeral director. There are certain rather strict divisions of authority and responsibility between them. The funeral director is in charge of bringing the body in and out of the church, arranging the procession (if there is one) to the church from the home and from the church to the cemetery. The minister is in charge when the funeral director turns over the service to him at the church until he gives the benediction again. The minister also has the authority of the church for telling the funeral director within what limits he may operate on church property. The minister will improve his own position if he does not interfere or meddle in matters which belong to the undertaker. If he is asked to ride to the cemetery in a certain car and can do so conveniently, he should agree to it, understanding that very often the undertaker in a rural community is burdened by friendly volunteers who wish to help the bereaved family, and that one way of assigning a significant responsibility to such a volunteer is to ask him to drive the minister. If the minister agrees for the most part to the funeral director's plans, the funeral director will be more ready to fit in with essential plans and requests of the minister. Minister and undertaker who understand each other and work together as a team will increase their individual helpfulness to bereaved persons.

14

The Pastor's Ministry in the Home

NO WORK of the minister is more important than that which he does in pastoring his people. It still is true that "a homegoing pastor makes a churchgoing people." Pastoral calling is important not only in its own right but also as an invaluable support of other phases of ministerial work. Administrative procedures are made at once more human and more realistic when the minister knows his people not only in their public roles but also in their private lives. Preaching becomes relevant to need and life when it grows out of the everyday purposeful contacts of the pastor with his people in the setting of their own homes and fields.

It has become somewhat fashionable to laugh at "ringing doorbells." Well, the rural pastor never did ring them; there were few doorbells where he called. If pastoral work be understood in terms of social calling of an afternoon, then it indeed deserves to be laughed at as beneath the dignity of the pastoral office. But pastoral work so understood is profoundly misunderstood. Pastoral calling is actually a systematic and comprehensive audit of the personal and familial resources and health of a parish, and a long term attempt to conserve and increase those resources in the light of the Christian gospel and in terms of the personalities of the parishioners.

Such pastoral work has three aspects which are never mutually exclusive and which constantly overlap, but which can be separated and treated distinctly for purposes of analysis. They are: routine calling, emergency calling, and counseling.

I shall discuss routine calling first because it is basic to the other two, and we shall be effective in these only as we are first effective in our routine calls. The first requirement in routine calling is that the pastor should set for himself a standard of achievement. That standard will vary with the family load of the parish, his other church responsibilities, and, to a certain extent, with his own physical condition. A minimum requirement would seem to be three calls on each family in the church constituency each year.

It is not enough, however, to have this general goal. The number of calls must be broken down to a weekly quota. If there are 250 families in the parish and we purpose to make 3 calls on each, then we must make a total of 750 routine calls each year.[1] If we eliminate vacation weeks, Christmas and Easter weeks, and the occasions when some general church responsibility such as teaching in a youth camp or attending annual conference takes us out of the local parish, we can count on something like forty weeks a year for systematic visitation. That means that we must make approximately 19 calls a week to make our 750 per year or 3 per family annually.

Then we must have a set time for calling—a time selected in relationship to our previously accepted goal of calls. Experience indicates that a rural pastor can average six calls in an afternoon. If we have to make nineteen routine calls a week, that will require three afternoons. We then set aside Tuesday, Thursday, and Friday afternoons from 1:30 to 5:30 for routine calling. And we see to it that no matter of personal convenience interferes with our accepted responsibility. Obviously funerals and special church and organizational meetings will interfere with such a schedule from time to time. We have allowed for a margin of interference by scheduling calling for only forty of the fifty-two weeks of the year. It also helps a busy pastor to keep up to schedule if he does not allow an early afternoon funeral or a late afternoon committee meeting to take the whole afternoon. Some calling can and should be done before and after these other obligations. Another means of keeping on schedule is not to stop

[1] It should be obvious that if the number of families goes beyond 400, the pastor must have assistance or reduce the annual quota of calls per family.

toward the end of the afternoon just because we have completed six calls. That is just the time to make the seventh and eighth against the afternoon when we are confronted with a situation so tense that we must devote the whole afternoon to a single home.

A third requirement is that we have a set route. Now this does not mean that we should always call on our parishioners in the same order, so that they know that we are expected every three months on the third Tuesday. Rather it means that we should map the roads on which our people live and then visit systematically up one road and down the next. Suppose we have a church in a small village around which our people live. We go out the north road to the farthest parishioner and then call right back along the road south, visiting each parishioner until we are back to town again. Then we take the northeast road, and so on. It is important to call on each family which belongs to or is sympathetic to the church without missing one, if we are doing routine calling. Our car is always recognized; and if we go by a home without stopping, we raise questions as to our attitude toward the family missed. We need not worry about this if we are calling on a single family in case of emergency, since the neighbors will know of the emergency anyhow and will understand why we visit one family without visiting others. When we have made one series of calls and are ready for the next, we vary our procedure by beginning not with the north road but with the west road. Thus our visiting is orderly and comprehensive, yet it is not so rigidly scheduled that people are able to predict our arrival and stage our visits.

Finally, for each round of calls the pastor should have a stated emphasis. Emphases should be selected for the whole year in planning the total program of the church so that they fit in with the other activities and strengthen them. One year, for instance, we might choose to emphasize the missionary program of the church in the autumn, leading up to Christmas season with its message of God's free gift of love to us. The devotional life of the family makes an appropriate winter

123

emphasis leading up to the Easter celebration of Christ's sacrifice on our behalf. In the spring we might appropriately give attention to the educational program of the church, including our church colleges, for at that time our young people graduating from high school are considering their future course.

In connection with each emphasis the pastor should make a careful general preparation so that he is widely conversant with the matter he wishes to present. If his preparation is narrow or rote, he will have only a sales talk to parrot from house to house. What he should bring instead is a broad concern for the interest he wishes to emphasize, which will enable him to relate the life of the family he is visiting to what he has to say. In this connection he should provide himself with some pamphlet literature which he can leave in the home to carry forward and enlarge the presentation he had been able to make. This literature should be varied so that he will not always leave the same piece of literature in each home.

Having set his standard of achievement, his schedule of work, his route, and his emphasis, the pastor is now ready to call. It should not be necessary to say that he should make pastoral calls alone. The habit of taking along one's wife on a series of pastoral calls is, to speak temperately, an unfortunate one. There are occasions when the pastor and his wife should call together, but these are not pastoral calls but social calls.

In a pastoral call we expect to talk seriously with the members of a family about the problems most important to them. We must always be ready and waiting to have individual persons unburden their hearts to us in confession. It is many times more difficult to talk to two persons than to one about a serious problem; if pastor and wife call together, it is almost assured that no existing tension will be uncovered by their visit. Sometimes the unfortunate practice of a predecessor leads our people to expect us to bring our wives with us in calling. I have found that a frank statement of my reason for calling alone is adequate to produce understanding and acceptance. I have said something like this in response to a question as to why my wife hadn't come too: "When I come to call as your

124

pastor I always expect that you may have some problem which you wish to talk over with me confidentially. My experience is that in every family sooner or later there comes a time when some member of that family wants special help and counsel. My experience also shows that a person can never talk as easily to two as he can to one. Because I want you to feel free to talk over any problem with me under the easiest possible of conditions, I come alone. On the other hand, Mrs. Smith and I love chicken and would be glad to come down for an evening's social visit together whenever you say the word." Over a period of years I have found such a statement was always well received, and we have accepted a multitude of invitations for dinner or supper as well.

Suppose we are now on our way early in the afternoon to begin our calling in a farm home. We are presenting the missionary program of the church as we call in this circuit of the parish. Remembering that men are the dominant group in the rural community, we are on the lookout for the man of the house as we drive up the highway and turn off on the farm lane. Perhaps we sight him running his tractor in the field bordering the road. At once we stop our car by the highway fence and wait until he reaches our end of the field so that we can greet him. A man at work ordinarily does not wish to be long interrupted, although upon occasion he will want to talk, and we must be alert to signs of this need. Our goal is to make this farmer feel that he is the head of the household in our thinking and that we begin our contact with the home by talking to him. An appreciative and understanding word about his crops or fields or machinery is an excellent beginning; or a question as to what he is doing, if we are honestly ignorant, is never amiss. Then an inquiry for the various members of the family is in order, leading naturally to the statement: "Well, I'll drive up to the house and see Mary and the children." It is important to avoid any implication that he should stop his work and join you; on rare occasions he may really wish to do so, but in general he will want to continue his work. An excellent practice is to have some piece of literature which you can leave with him to stick in his overall pocket and read while he is resting.

We now drive on to the farmyard. Leaving our car we walk up to the door, and the choice of doors may prove a very important matter. Always use the door which seems most evidently in use by members of the household and neighbors, the one to which the worn path leads. Generally this will be a rear or side door. Often the front entrance is never used. In one northern state a pastor stood waiting for admittance at the front door while on the inside his winter-bound parishioners removed the nails with which the entrance had been made tight against the searching winds. Needless to say, that call was profitless except as it taught that pastor a lesson.

It is always wise as well as courteous to follow the lead of the person who greets us at the door. Many pastors wishing to be no trouble to the busy housewife insist on sitting down in the kitchen in order that she may go on with her work. There is no harm in showing a willingness so to do; but if she insists that we go into the living room, wisdom dictates that we go. Perhaps she is tired of her house chores and ready and eager to make this visit an occasion for a rest on her part. Perhaps she has something about which she wishes counsel and wants to give her entire attention to the conversation under relaxing conditions such as the kitchen does not permit. In many farm homes the bathroom adjoins the kitchen and some member of the family may be trapped there, unable to make his escape to the bedroom for more adequate clothing as long as you are in the kitchen. There are so many untoward possibilities in the situation that it is politic to go where we are asked to go, even if that appears on the surface to be putting the family to some trouble.

If there is a choice in chairs to be taken, the pastor is wise who does not take the most comfortable seat. Ministers are often accused of customarily taking the best place simply because it is so often given to them. Where we have an option, let us exert it in taking a humble station. When we are seated, however, it is very important that we take a position which

126

indicates that we are comfortable and enjoying ourselves. We shall see that twenty minutes to half an hour is plenty of time in which to make a helpful call. Many ministers who stay an hour or more still have reputations for being in a hurry simply because they sit on the edges of their chairs and act ill at ease during the entire course of their visit. The impression that we have made only a short and hurried call is determined not by the actual time we spend but by the leisurely or the hurried attitude we show. An attitude of complete but attentive relaxation is conducive to the best use of the limited time we have.

Again a word of appreciation of home or furnishings is a good start for the conversation. But to make this statement of appreciation routine so that we say the same thing over and over again on each succeeding call is not only to be ineffective but to be insincere. It is well to use the early minutes of the call to ask questions about the children and their progress in school or to get up-to-date information upon family members living away from the neighborhood. In all of this questioning it is not, of course, the simple facts that we are after; a comprehensive inventory of the family members will tell us, through the reactions of our hostess, whether family tensions have arisen. If in response to our question about an older daughter now away from home she suddenly becomes indefinite, embarrassed, and confused, we may reasonably conclude that there is some family difficulty in relationship to that child and give the mother an opening to talk about it.

In this connection a pastor should always be ready to discard his special emphasis if he senses tension in the family and deal with that tension as directly as he can. The plan to talk about missions should never so fill his mind that he becomes blind to a real missionary need in the immediate family he is addressing. To have a specific purpose in a round of calls is to avoid the banality and the pointlessness that so much of our visiting has; but this specific purpose must never blind us to our deeper function as pastors, which is to care for the members of our flock in terms of their most intimate needs.

Let us suppose, however, that our early conversation indicates no serious emotional tensions, and we are ready to begin our presentation of the missionary program of the church. We look around the room and note on top of the bookcase a picture of a man in uniform—a younger brother of the wife. "Where did Eddie serve?" we ask. And upon receiving this information we follow it up in an easy and natural transition to a presentation of the missionary challenge in the particular land where Eddie served. Such a book as Henry P. Van Dusen's *They Found the Church There* will provide us with excellent illustrative materials. Suppose, however, Eddie never got abroad but served entirely in this country; then the way is opened for a discussion of home missions and then foreign missions as a natural continuation. At the end of our call we have tied the outgoing evangelistic world crusade of the church into the ongoing life of that farm home.

Whatever literature we plan to leave is best given at the end of our call. Indeed, it may be well not to carry the literature into the home but to go back to the car to get it when we are leaving. One of the children can come with us to carry it back to the house, or we can step back to the door ourselves with whatever we choose to leave. To leave literature in this fashion makes the gift not a routine passing out of propaganda but an individualized provision of materials for further study to an already interested family. It is a good practice to red-pencil literature at points which particularly bear out the interests indicated in the prior conversation.

What about pastoral prayer in connection with a routine call? Many of us come to shy away from praying with our people because we have felt that such a prayer was artificially and formally tacked on to our call. Quite clearly if this is the case we ought not to pray, because to pray under such circumstances is to make the life of Christian experience unreal to the family we are trying to help. But our feeling as to the artificiality of prayer in a calling situation may be due to two

128

factors which demand our thoughtful consideration as pastors. One of these is our own insensitivity to human need—we do not pray because we do not see how tremendous the need of that particular family is and how powerless we are by and of ourselves to meet it. The second is that we have a low or superstitious view of prayer—we do not understand prayer as the lifting of our problems and our fellowship to the level of fellowship with God.

Certainly we should pray with our people if they ask us to pray. Probably we should pray with them if we have discussed some problem of importance to members of the family or if we have been celebrating some special joy or good fortune. Not to pray in either of these cases is to fail to bring to the family the resources we have as pastors. However, the decision to have prayer should in general be made by the family. We can ask, "Would you like to have me say a word of prayer with you now?" On occasion such a request will meet with a somewhat fumbling answer. Anything short of a definite negative should be taken as a positive approval. Should the family refuse our request, that ends the matter; there is then a very good reason for not praying, a reason which suggests that we should repeat our call in this home in the immediate future. Most pastors now do not kneel to pray with a family although there are some regions in which kneeling is still the custom. When we are seated at the kitchen table or in the living room or standing in the doorway, our prayer takes on the natural unaffected qualities which characterize Christian experience and rural life at their best.

A good pastor is one who knows how to leave when he starts to leave. One of the acts that has made pastoral calls unpopular among our laymen has been our tendency to announce our departure and then go on talking. When we say, "I am going now," let us immediately head for the door. If our attitude has been relaxed during our call, our people will not feel that we have only been there a short time. If we call regularly, a twenty-minute to half-hour call is quite long enough to take care of the business at hand.

In all routine calling the pastor must work with tact and a sense of humor. Often his first vital contact will come from the call he does not make. When he arrives to call and finds everyone dressed up and obviously just ready to leave for town, good sense indicates that he should recognize the situation, pay his respects to the family, and urge them to go on about their projected excursion while he visits at the next neighbor's. If he knows his families and their trading habits well, he will not call on days when they are apt to be going out; but when occasionally he does find such a situation, he commends his cause by making a rapid and tactful exit.

Children on their home grounds are often prone to acts and words which embarrass their parents. The pastor who can and does remain unruffled and unshocked by childish misbehavior, naughtiness, or candor will win the hearts of both parents and children. Most children misbehave to attract attention to themselves, and we can avoid many difficulties by paying attention to the children at the start so that they will not feel under the necessity of purchasing our interest by unusual or unhappy acts. Incidentally, the friendly pastor who reaches out to the children and is never shocked by things they do will find that when, in a very short space of time, these children become adolescents they will come to him for help with their pressing problems. He who wishes to help youth and adults must begin to help them when they are children.

The Pastor's Ministry to the Sick

IN 1939 I made a study of Wisconsin rural families chosen to represent the best in the piety of their several churches. Roman Catholic, Lutheran, and Evangelical church families were visited in relatively equal numbers and asked a variety of questions having to do with their relationship to the church and the community. As might have been expected there was a great diversity in the answers to the various questions not only in the whole group but within the various denominational subgroups. On only one answer was there unanimity. When asked under what conditions they would call their pastor to visit in their homes, all families listed sickness as an appropriate cause for summoning him. Apparently families who are most effectively indoctrinated in the tenets of the various denominations agree universally that the crisis of sickness is one better faced with the aid of a spiritual counselor. It was somewhat disconcerting to discover that only a third of these same families reported that their pastor did call in case of sickness. Here the pastors were certainly not taking advantage of a door thrown open to them in the lives of their people.

Obviously within the slender confines of this volume there can be no comprehensive treatment of our ministry to the sick. For such a treatment the student must turn to the excellent specialized treatises listed in the bibliography. My aim here will be simply to suggest the place of a sick visitation program in the total work of a minister and to list certain practices to be used or avoided. In all of this I insist that nowhere has the minister a more real human responsibility or opportunity and that he ought to prepare himself to be of the highest service by assiduous calling on the sick and by taking advantage of some of the excellent clinical training courses available through the Council for Clinical Training Inc., Cambridge, Mass.

Any sickness which disables or removes an individual from his work represents a major personal crisis for him. It often represents a major familial crisis as well. Whenever we face a crisis there is a tendency deep within us to come back to first things, to the ultimate and all-important issues of life. A man whose attitude toward his responsibilities has been careless and casual may, under the pressure of sickness with its sudden and dramatic change of life situation, its pain, its enforced idleness, and its fears, suddenly become intensely concerned with life's ultimate meaning. The height of his concern will often be in inverse proportion to his earlier indifference, for the indifferent man has no answer to life's pressing questions when he confronts them. Even the deeply religious man may find himself lost when sickness comes, often because his religion, so satisfying in other situations, now no longer yields him the peace his mind craves.

For the family sickness means the loss of the breadwinner and in many cases the loss of income as well; or it means the loss of the homemaker with all the adjustments of living arrangements that involves. Even when some other family member than father or mother is the sick person, the whole complex pattern of family relationships is changed; that the sick family member is a child ought never lead us to the conclusion that his condition does not affect the family pattern. Often a child carries much more of an emotional and psychological freight in the family than his years or his capabilities suggest to the outsider.

Every sickness represents a life crisis; but psychosomatic medicine reminds us that some sicknesses also represent the attempt of an individual to meet a life crisis. There may be a flight into sickness by which situations which are intolerable to the person are avoided or changed. And such sickness is physically a real thing, it is not malingering. There are people who solve problems by breaking bones. Even an accidental injury may have its deepest roots in emotional tension. It

132

scarcely needs to be pointed out that where organic sickness has developed in meeting a personal need, a substantial return to real health waits upon the patient's coming to terms with his underlying problem. Here you and I as pastors have our main business.

In the rural community the fabric of social life is much more closely woven than in the city. Where people are relatively few and relationships relatively intense, disabling sickness makes a more serious rent in the social fabric—the incapacity of one person counts heavily. This fact presents on the one hand a problem to be met: sick calls will involve a special ministry to family and neighborhood as well as to the sick person; the pastor will find himself with surprising frequency telephoning a neighbor to report on John's condition at the hospital. On the other hand, it offers a resource to be counted on and used. Concerned neighbors can and do take care of the emergency work and shopping needs of a family whose breadwinner is temporarily incapacitated. The minister should expect this sort of service and point out needs for it wherever and whenever they are overlooked.

Because of the population structure of rural society and its occupational characteristics the rural pastor must expect to have a great deal of service to render to certain types of illness and incapacity. The high rural birth rate means a correspondingly large number of persons involved in childbirth with its triumphs and tragedies. Where children are so numerous, the diseases of childhood will abound. Among our most dangerous occupations are farming and mining, and the minister must expect to deal with relatively frequent accidental injuries. Finally, the high proportion of aged persons means that he will have much to do with the diseases of senility and what hospitals call terminal sicknesses.

There are certain preparations which the pastor ought to make before visiting the sick. First of all is his physical preparation. He needs to be in good physical health himself before he ventures to minister to others who are in poor health. Obviously a minister with a cold, a sore throat, or a headache ought not to call upon sick persons. His own attitudes under such circumstances will depress those whom he tries to serve, and there is always the chance that his physical illness will be spread by his visit so that the ultimate physical state of those to whom he is ministering will be made worse. Furthermore he needs to be clean. Sick people are particularly sensitive to dirt. Offensive odors of sweat, tobacco, and bad breath should be guarded against. Dirty fingernails, soiled linen, a spotted vest are all avoidable and should be avoided. Of course the pastor ought to be physically clean at all times; but nowhere is this so important as when we are visiting sick people.

There is an intellectual preparation which the minister should make. He needs definitely to know how ill the person is on whom he is calling. If it is a hospital case, he can find out about the patient by talking to the head nurse on the floor. Indeed he should never think of entering a hospital room without first having checked with the floor nurse not only as to the patient's condition but as to his acceptability as a caller at the moment. The pastor who heedlessly pushes into sickrooms without the counsel of the nurse will sooner or later be needlessly embarrassed. And his parishioners will be constantly embarrassed. From the nurse he can find out how the patient feels, how long a visit he will enjoy, whether he has had drugs or opiates which will cause confusion in conversation, above all what his general and dominating attitude is. On the basis of this information and his own knowledge of the family situation and the person himself immediately concerned, he can chart out a course of action which will prove positively helpful.

Should the sick person be at home—as is so often the case in rural areas—unless he is being cared for by a trained nurse, information about his condition must be secured directly from the physician who is caring for him. The pastor need feel no embarrassment at telephoning or visiting the office of a doctor for the purpose of securing information about the sick in his parish. The pastor will be more welcome when he does come for information if he has previously sought out the local doctor, made his acquaintance, and suggested his interest in the physical health of persons in the community. The doctor who knows the minister as an ally in health education and public health action will naturally be ready to trust him with medical information about his parishioners.

Sometimes we serve as ministers in areas so isolated from health services that there is no doctor to consult. Even then we should attempt from members of the family to get as adequate a picture as possible of the patient's condition before calling on him. Moreover should such a condition of isolation from medical service exist, we as community leaders have a responsibility for leading community opinion and action to the end of securing something like normal medical service. Even among relatively poor families some sort of medical prepayment plan along the line of those worked out by the Farm Security Administration (now The Farmers Home Administration) is possible and should be developed.

Should the ill person be hospitalized in a city at some distance from his home, as is often the case, it is the part of good sense to call or visit his family for information before going to the hospital. A farmer's physical illness may be complicated with worry over how his stock is faring while he is away. The assurance that his sons have the farm in hand and that the stock looks fine is the best kind of medicine. A mother's joy over the birth of a child may be dulled by apprehension as to the care being given the other children. A factual report may ease her mind so that she can enter into a fuller enjoyment of her new motherhood.

And there is a spiritual preparation for calling on the sick. Not even at the altar of the church does the minister stand more for the mercy and love of God than as he enters the sickroom. Such a responsibility is not to be accepted in man's strength alone. Only a full discipline of prayer will enable the pastor to stand for God as he should. Our Lord in connection with his healing of the epileptic boy advised his disciples:

135

"This kind can come forth by nothing, but by prayer and fasting." No sick call should be made until the pastor has tried to see the sick man and his problems through the eyes of God. Only the pastor who has opened his life to the guidance of the Holy Spirit in each particular case will discharge the responsibility of a pastor to the sick.

There are several serious mistakes to be avoided at all cost in the sickroom. First, never whisper in the presence of or near a sick person. Always speak in low tones which he can hear perfectly. Occasionally members of the family will start to whisper some special information to you. Silence them at once with a gesture and motion them to come out of the house or down the corridor out of earshot to talk. A sick person easily becomes suspicious; he thinks that people are trying to fool him and that he is much worse off than they tell him he is. When he hears the sibilance of whispering he indubitably concludes that others are saying what they do not want him to hear because it would discourage him. Fear then does a worse work than actual bad news about his condition would do. Under no circumstances whisper or permit others to whisper to you in the presence or in earshot of a sick person.

Second, have as little as you can decently have to do with any deception of the patient. There is a real ethical question as to whether the modern practice of keeping the seriousness of a sickness from the sick person is just or kind. After all, this life is his own, and when any force threatens it or seems to be bringing it to a speedy close, he is entitled to all the facts. There is no kindness in permitting a man to waste what may be crucial last days for him. And there is no evidence for the assumption that ordinary human beings will go to pieces when told that they are in serious peril or close to death. On the other hand when doctor and family have conspired together to deceive the patient, we have no right to assume the responsibility of overriding their decision. Should the patient under such circumstances ask us, "Am I going to get well?" our answer may well be, "I'm not a physician and have no basis for telling you one way or the other." This opens the way for him to speak about the fears that are his real concern.

Third, never speak in the presence of a sick person on the assumption that he is unconscious and cannot hear the conversation. Human consciousness is a tricky business at best, and what often passes for a lack of consciousness on the part of a sick person is actually mere inability to express reaction. A young wife in a hospital, fighting to recover from a desperate and radical operation, lay in apparent unconsciousness on her bed. Beside her an interne and two nurses discussed their appraisal of her chances of recovery. They were all pessimistic about her ability to continue to live. This whole conversation was overheard by the sick woman. By not even the flicker of an eyelid was she able to indicate her awareness, yet the bitter struggle she was making for life received a fresh hindrance from those employed to help her. Fortunately she recovered and eventually could talk about the experience, but there are doubtless many who have gone down to death overridden by the thoughtless speculations of persons who should have supported their struggle for life.

Now let us assume we are ready to make our call. A cardinal rule to remember in all we do in the sickroom is to refrain from being a burden or a responsibility to the sick person. To that end we should leave hat and overcoat in the cloakroom or hall before entering the room. If there is nothing to do but take them with us, then as soon as we enter we can unobtrusively place them on the floor at the side of the room or on an empty chair.

Our greeting to the sick person is important. It should be friendly and happy without a boisterousness or effusiveness that offends by its very contrast with the patient's own weakened condition. It should not call for more of an answer than the patient feels readily able to give. Any greeting that asks him for an extended commentary on his own physical condition is unfortunate. There come times when the patient will want to talk about his operation or condition at length, but he should bring the matter up himself. "Hello, Jim," is quite greeting enough.

Often we are asked to call upon a sick person whom we have not previously known. Here an informal greeting is of course inappropriate. It is best to introduce ourselves immediately and explain our presence in terms of the one who told us of the patient's sickness and asked us to call. We might say, "Mrs. Hill, I'm the Methodist preacher in town and found out from the head nurse that you're a Methodist. I stopped by to get acquainted and to see if there is anything you'd like to have me do for you." Sometimes under such circumstances we discover that this patient is really a member of the parish of a brother minister who should have been called in our place. When this is the case we should make as much of a pastoral call as the immediate situation indicates, assure the patient that we are notifying her pastor, and then notify him by telephone or personal call the same day. It goes without saying that when we receive such a notification from a brother minister we will go at once to the hospital and make the necessary call.

Beyond the initial greeting each call should follow its own pattern. With a desperately ill person we may only step to the side of the bed, take his hand, recite a few appropriate words of scripture, and offer a short prayer. Even when the patient is unconscious, we should remember the possibility of his hearing us and offer a short prayer with him. In an astonishing number of cases he will later thank us for a thoughtfulness and concern which at the time we thought him powerless to appreciate. It is well to remember that seriously ill persons can grasp only a few and simple ideas. An appropriate scripture verse simple and brief enough for a drugged mind to grasp and repeat again and again may be a strength in dark hours. One of the great skills which a pastor develops only with long years of experience is the suggestion of scripture verses which meet the pressing need of the sick man or woman for fundamental assurance.

In the case of a convalescent the call will be longer and

THE PASTOR'S MINISTRY TO THE SICK

will follow the more usual pattern of our calls. In particular we should listen for indications of guilt feelings or depression. We do not serve the patient well when we offer him easy comfort and assurance. What he more often needs is a patient counselor who will help him bring the vague feeling of boredom or confusion or despair to the surface of his mind and accept them. To that end we ought to listen a great deal in our sick calls, limiting our conversation to indications of our acceptance and appreciation of the patient and on no account arguing with him.

Sick calls should almost always end with prayer—again, prayer with the permission of the patient. To fail to give an opportunity for prayer is to withhold from the patient the unique ministry he expects of us. Indeed unless we give him an opportunity for prayer, he may feel that we regard his case as either morally or physically so hopeless that we refuse to pray for him. The only exception to be made to the rule of asking permission of the patient to pray is when we are ministering to an extremely sick man who ought not to be asked to make any decisions. In his case we simply announce that we are going to pray with him; sometimes all we need to do is to recite a scripture verse or verses and then begin to pray.

All of us are aware of the danger implicit in certain types of prayer with the sick. Sometimes marginally religious persons feel that if the minister comes to pray with them, they must be almost on the brink of death. That impression has been fostered and increased by the positively immoral practice of certain sectarian groups who make sickness the occasion for emotional appeals for repentance and conversion. Calls and prayers by ministers addicted to this approach often terrorize or at least excite or depress the patient. In situations where this type of ministry has been common, prayer at the bedside may be easily misunderstood. Caution should characterize our use of prayer wherever we suspect that this sort of ministry has been active. However, if our prayer be Christian—that is, if it be in the name and spirit of Jesus—and if prayer is not the occasional emergency practice of our ministry but the constant climax of it, our prayers will not for long or in general be misunderstood.

Among the central problems of the sick person is the problem of death. One of the tragic weaknesses of our age is its unwillingness or inability to come to grips with the fact of death. As medical science has pushed death farther away from us in time, we have acted as if the postponement of death meant that we could safely overlook or disregard its inevitability. As a result even deeply religious persons are unprepared to die. The church through its preaching and teaching ministries ought again to interpret the meaning of death to our people and to prepare them with Christian attitudes in advance of their own physical dissolution. In the meantime we have to deal with persons who face death entirely unprepared for it.

The pastor can be of help in his basic attitude. He must accustom himself to suffering and to the general ugliness of wasting sickness so that he will show no sign of distress or aversion when he enters the presence of an extremely sick or dying man. Such a person is isolated at best, he is struggling alone against a mysterious enemy in his disease. If his pastor treats him with even a suggestion of distaste or hesitation, his isolation will only be increased by the visit. What he needs to feel in his sickness is that amid change, confusion, and even dissolution there are certain constants which do not alter.

And here, of course, is one of the dividends of routine pastoral calling. Our parishioners are used to having us come to them, they have received us before, not once but again and again. When we enter the sickroom, the sick man is at once thrown into an old familiar situation. Perhaps he looks up to say, "Preacher, I never thought you'd see me in as bad a shape as this!" If we have been visiting him regularly as his pastor, we can reply, "Why, Jim, I've seen you in all kinds of situations—on the tractor, nursing a sick cow, digging out the lane after a blizzard, worrying when Martha was so sick. Why are

140

you so concerned about my seeing you like this?" In the light of his memory of old fellowship he can gather strength to look at his fears, even the fear of death itself.

As pastors we need constantly to be aware that the fear of death is not a single or a simple thing. It may involve any or several of the following: fear of an unknown future, fear of eternal punishment for sin, fear of losing the fellowship of married partner or other family member, fear of never being able to make up to some person for a real or imagined injury we have done him, fear of leaving a family unprovided for economically, fear of what will happen to an aged parent or a crippled or mentally retarded child when we are gone. And the list might be extended. The point is that the fear of death is not an unusual or different kind of fear but represents exactly the same kind of anxieties with which we are constantly forced to deal throughout our lives. The pastor's role is twofold: to help the dying person to recognize what his true fear is and to deal with it as objectively and realistically as he can; to help him to find such a fellowship with God as will allow him confidently to trust in that fellowship for all the uncertainties of every tomorrow.

Rural life, we must remember, is characterized by its wholeness. To rural people death is not an event divorced from the other aspects of life; most of them have seen their neighbors die and have helped to care for the dying. Death is part of the natural process which they observe in the seasons, in their crops and livestock, and in themselves. The pastor must beware lest he import his own fears of death into his parishioner's situation. He may often find that the man whom he came to comfort has an attitude and a wisdom in the face of death which will comfort his pastor. We should be ready to weep with those who weep, but we fail as pastors if we are not ready to appreciate the insight and faith of our parishioners and to rejoice with those who rejoice in facing the uncertain future with the certain God.

In this chapter I have offered an outline of the place of calling on the sick in relationship to the total work of the ministry. For the content of sick calling the pastor should consult the several excellent books listed in the bibliography. Most of all he ought to consult his own experience as a pastor to sick people and learn from his mistakes as well as his successes how the healing and the mercy of God may be mediated to suffering men. No task of the ministry will make a man more humble and none will do more to make his own religious experience vital.

The Pastor's Ministry to the Bereaved

BEREAVEMENT is a psychological and spiritual condition little understood, because we are naturally apt to focus our attention on the fact of loss whereas the critical problem is what remains. Bereavement is not a different kind of experience; it is precisely the same sort of experience as any major parting. A son leaves for college; a daughter marries and moves to a distant state; a husband leaves for emergency diplomatic service abroad; a young couple leave their friends and home for missionary service in the Far East. In all of these experiences we have the more or less long-term severing of deep personal interdependencies. They differ from the separation brought on by the death of a loved person in that communication by mail or telephone is still possible and that an earthly reunion may still be contemplated.

We are all familiar, however, with the fact that long-term separations involve the persons separated in radical personal readjustments. Habits developed and achieved in the former relationship must now be painfully redirected and remade. Satisfactions supplied by the old relationship must now be discovered in some other direction. The rearrangement of old habit patterns is distressing to the person whose habits are thus disrupted. The search for new satisfactions may put demands upon other individuals which alter the whole pattern of the intimate social group. And this process with which we are so familiar in connection with human separations is precisely the same process which is at work in the life of a bereaved person and his family circle.

In urban life individuals are involved in a network of groups. Bereavement in such a setting tends less to break the accustomed pattern of our work and economic and social lives. Bad as we may feel, we are not reminded at every social turn of our loss. The city's impersonality gives us some relief from being bereaved and different. In the rural community we cannot do necessary shopping and engage in work or play without being met with reminders that we are bereaved. The grocer offers his condolences; the butcher tells us of when he lost his first wife; the ex-serviceman who fills the gas tank of the car has his anecdote to tell about our loved one; every contact re-establishes our status as alone. Nor are the specialized institutions of urban life available to serve us. In rural society most specialized service functions are met by the family. Our personal loss is accompanied by all kinds of real privations and inconveniences.

Let us take as an example a grandmother, sixty-seven years of age, suddenly bereaved of her husband. They have been farm people and were at the time of his sudden death still operating a large and successful farm. In the community live their four children. The oldest son operates a garage in the nearby village. The second child in the family, a daughter, lives with her husband on a neighboring farm. The third child, an unmarried daughter, is a schoolteacher in a city thirty-five miles away and maintains her home with her mother except during the school term. The youngest child, a son, has just returned from the army and married; he is studying under the G.I. Bill of Rights at the state university. The family has always been a completely harmonious one with the in-laws happy and at home in the old parental home. No friction between mother and daughter-in-law or son-in-law has ever developed.

Prior to her husband's death the mother had satisfied a whole series of deep personal needs through him. Her basic economic needs found their satisfaction in his efforts; food and clothing and shelter plus all the intricate arrangements that go with their procurement were the product of his efforts. Psychological needs also found their satisfaction in him; he was someone to talk to, to feel toward, to expect and anticipate reactions from. Social needs were satisfied in him;

144

she was known in the community as Ed Jones's wife, her position with regard to the total neighborhood and community pattern was determined in relationship to him. Finally, her sexual needs found satisfaction in him. Of course, aside from sexual needs, we would not maintain that all the other needs were exclusively satisfied by her husband, but the basic pattern of their satisfaction was determined by him.

Now all these needs are unsatisfied, and this woman must look around her for persons with whom she can re-establish a pattern of satisfactions. Her most natural course is to turn to the other members of her family. Let us follow the process through in connection with her economic need. Her husband has left her a life interest in his estate, and she is actually economically independent in terms of resources. But resources require management if they are to produce, and she is confronted with a management problem at once. Under such circumstances she may well turn to her oldest child for assistance. Now suddenly he finds himself not only responible for his own business in town but for his father's farm as well. Even though he is able to get a good man to do the farm work (and efficient farm hands are tragically scarce just now), the extensive supervision, planning, and legal arrangements fall upon him. And they do not fall upon him alone but they fall upon his entire family. Time which formerly he spent with them in family jaunts, picnics, movies, and parties, he now spends in conferences with his mother, in tours of the farm fields, or in visits to the judge's chambers or the lawyer's office.

The burden of all this falls upon his wife and his children. She would have to be a very wise and understanding wife indeed who did not feel neglected and left out in such a situation. And it is only natural for her not to blame her husband for the neglect but to blame her mother-in-law. Thus the stage is set for family frictions which may harden into a persistent family rift and even a broken home. Many of us as pastors have seen mother-in-law and daughter-in-law who had maintained a reputation for peace and harmony over the years suddenly become little better than dogs at each other's throats when the death of the mother's husband made them rivals for the time and attention of her son.

Here is certainly a situation in which the pastor should serve if he can. A little consideration will make it clear that we cannot deal directly with the mother and son. They are too emotionally bound up in the immediate fact of bereavement to heed reason. But the daughter-in-law stands emotionally insulated from the situation in its early stages. She is the one party to it who can afford a dispassionate view. Suppose, once we sense which way the tide of dependence is moving, that we make our approach to the daughter-in-law. We take occasion to call on her at a time when we can visit with her alone. We say something like this: "Mary, have you thought about the strain that Eddie will be bearing the next six months because of his dad's death? His mother is turning to him to help settle up the estate, and he'll have to manage the farm for awhile. That will mean long extra hours of work since his garage is pushing him as things are. It'll mean less time for fun and relaxation. Unless someone looks out for him especially, he'll wear himself out emotionally and physically. You're the one who can help him out, and I think you as his wife and I as his pastor ought to enter into a little conspiracy against Ed. Let's plan to get him out to a picnic or the movies at least once a week so he'll have a real chance to relax."

If we make this approach successfully to the son's wife, we effectively insure her against feeling neglect and bitterness because she is provided with a reasonable interpretation of her husband's preoccupation and a program of action for helping him. She now feels not frustration and resentment against her mother-in-law but active pride in her ability to help both her husband and his mother. And if resentments do not develop in her we have an opportunity to work reasonably with the other parties to the relationship. We can allow the widow to express her deep emotional need of dependence to us in pastoral interviews. We can point out, as she comes to see her need, the advantages of being economically independent with her funds cared for by the local bank so that she can be free to make a unique contribution of time and energy to the church such as she was not able to make while she had the responsibility of the farm home. Then we can provide for her such work in the church as will effectually give scope for developing new sources of psychological and social satisfaction.

What we have traced through in terms of economic dependence might similarly be followed in the psychological or social fields. It is extremely important to understand and handle the forces of psychological need which might permanently enslave the younger son or the unmarried daughter to their mother. Every rural community supplies examples of bitter, unhappy individuals who have never developed to their maturity because they were forced to become psychological foils for a widowed mother. What is needed is an interpretation of the situation pattern to the individual involved together with constant practical work with the widow to help her establish a normal readjustment.

We do not have any very clear data as to how real and pressing the sexual need may be in such a case as we have been discussing. It is established that sexual desire does not in all cases die out either with the menopause or with age. Obviously there is no direct course of action any of us can take to satisfy a possible sexual drive in the bereaved individual. However, we can see to it that these other needs are met and work on the assumption that the individual, the majority of whose needs are recognized and ministered to, will be able herself to handle the remaining unsatisfied needs. At this point we have certain negative indications. Whenever an older widowed woman runs off with or marries an unsuitable younger man, there is almost always a prior history of general neglect and disregard of her personal and social needs. In lonely and disregarded persons sexual drives have an opportunity to assert themselves incessantly and eventually lead to ill-advised action. To help the individual person to maintain a socially active and helpful life in the community is to insure him or her against undue pressure from a possible sexual drive.

On the other hand suppose it is the wife who dies, leaving her seventy-two-year-old husband. What are the unresolved needs we meet here? Three of them—the psychological, the social, and the sexual—are the same. In the case of the widower the economic need is replaced by the domestic one. What a man needs is not someone to manage his business but someone to cook his meals, clean his home, and darn his socks. And the widowed farmer is particularly vulnerable at this point. He is used to coming in from the field to find a warm meal waiting for him. He gets up in the morning, goes to his dresser drawer, and finds a clean pair of overalls there. But now that his wife is gone, this old familiar pattern is all changed. Cold meals, dirty linen, a mussy house—all conspire to unsettle and disturb even the most stable man. Many of the quick and unhappy marriages which take place between older men and young women in the countryside are due to the fact that a man eventually becomes desperate and will do anything in hope of a clean house and warm meals again.

Why cannot we as pastors call in the group resources of the neighborhood and the church in meeting this domestic need? Neighbors reminded of a man's loneliness will be glad to have him in for warm meals. The woman's society could well organize committees to tend to housecleaning over a period of weeks or months. And the pastor can often find a woman ready to care for man's laundry at a modest fee. What is needed is not people to do the necessary work but some organizing central personality to give the work purpose and direction. The pastor can and should be that organizing center.

If the emergencies of domestic arrangements are cared for, there is a real expectation that a bereaved man will be able to deal creatively with his loneliness. Here the pastor who fishes or hunts will have a decided advantage. Many a man has been able to bring out into the open and face his desperate feeling of loneliness as he chatted with his pastor sitting in the opposite end of the rowboat and waiting for a strike. The essential requirement is that the bereaved individual not be left alone but be given such opportunities for friendly contact and fellowship as will allow him to unburden himself.

In connection with bereavement we have dealt with its meaning for older persons. A word is in order about the fact of death and children. There is a dangerous school of thought which, honestly eager to protect children from emotional shock, urges that since they cannot understand death, they ought to be isolated from it as much as possible. This course will result in the development of fears and insecurities far beyond any that come from a frank facing of the fact of death. That the dead relative or parent is gone we cannot conceal from the child. If he feels that his questions are met with evasion and concealment on the part of those he loves and trusts, he cannot but come to the conclusion that there is something shameful and wrong in the situation. He will then speculate upon this in secret or, unable to face it, repress the whole matter to the unconscious from whence it will find expression in nightmares, phobias, and the whole train of neurotic symptoms.

Of great advantage in dealing with this situation is the wholeness which characterizes rural life and which at this point is on the side of emotional health. Children in the rural community hear death talked about by neighbors. They listen in naturally on conversations of their elders. When bereavement strikes at the child, he cannot be isolated from it as the segmentalism of urban life allows. He is confronted with the fact of the death of his loved one in the attitude and words of everyone he meets. They know that he has suffered a loss; they take an attitude toward him which reflects this knowledge, and they expect him to react emotionally to his loss. What may seem to us at first an unfeeling cruelty which looks for signs of grief in a child may actually help him in giving him the security of a role to play and an attitude to hold in a hitherto uncharted situation.

149

Often our desire to protect a child in bereavement is simply our own unwillingness to face the fact of death and our desire to forget about the whole matter and not to think about it enough to be able to talk to the child about it. Obviously this point of view is understandable, but no one would regard it as mature or Christian. Children should be given every opportunity to satisfy their curiosity about death even to touching the body of the dead person, though that may seem distasteful to us. They should be permitted to ask, and to have answers to, all the questions they desire, even though our answers may seem unsatisfactory. What is important to the child is not a logically airtight answer to a question but an assurance that persons he loves have some answer for him and are ready to entertain his queries. The worst possible procedure is to deceive the child about death with the evasion that the loved person has gone away, as if there would be some earthly return.

For adults no less than for children there is no easy or acceptable explanation of death. It is one of the facts with which limited men and women must come to grips. The Christian gospel is a good news about death as well as about life. It assures us that the love of God which we know in Jesus is the constant of our experience no matter what that experience may be. Even at the dead ends of life when other resources and securities are unavailing, that Love is present and we rest in it. Our business as pastors is to help our people to the security of that Love.

The Pastor's Ministry as Counselor

DURING the last fifteen years the movement to do intensive personal work with individuals or small groups has gained a great momentum in educational and religious circles under the name of counseling or guidance. The roots of the movement are diverse: previous work by pastors—particularly hospital chaplains—with troubled people, the vocational counseling movement in the schools and colleges, work with problem children in school situations, and the rise of the dynamic psychological understanding of human nature due to the insights of Freud and subsequent psychoanalysts and psychiatrists. All of us need to understand that modern counseling is an attempt to do systematically and with scientific understanding what pastors down through the centuries have been doing on the basis of common sense. Counseling provides new tools for an old task.

In the beginning of this discussion a few terms need to be defined in the interest of avoiding error and misunderstanding. Psychiatry is the medical art of diagnosing and prescribing treatment for the mentally ill. Psychiatrists are physicians—that is, men who have earned the M.D. degree—who practice this art as a specialty. Psychoanalysis is a theory of the nature and the treatment of mental illness stemming from the pioneer work of Sigmund Freud. Psychoanalysts are persons who accept the main outlines of this theory and aim at curing mentally ill persons by applying the method. They are generally medical doctors in which case they are also called psychiatrists, but psychoanalysis makes room for the use of the method by persons not M.D.'s so that every psychoanalyst is not necessarily a psychiatrist. There are lay analysts whose training does not include a medical degree. Psychotherapy is the art of healing the mentally ill persons by interview and expression rather than drugs, physical treatments, or surgery. It is comparable to physical therapy or occupational therapy in the treatment of illness. It is often given by a psychiatrist but may be given by a person who is not an M.D. just as the various other types of treatments are given by persons not professional physicians.

From the above definitions it is clear that the pastor is not a psychiatrist or a psychoanalyst or a psychotherapist, although he may profit by insights and interpretations of the structure and dynamics of personality garnered from the work and research of these men. He ought to understand enough about the maladjustments of personality to know when to refer his parishioners to the care of these experts. The most helpful pastor is he who knows the limits of his own competence and turns for help to other specialists when dealing with serious personal disorganization. It is particularly important for a pastor to understand something of the nature of major psychological disturbances, because they often are framed in religious phraseology and have their onset in a period of intense religious concern. Danger signs which suggest the need of psychiatric care and treatment include:

1. Marked divergences in character traits from previous known characteristics, such as a sober man beginning to drink.

2. Withdrawal from activities of a social nature, refusal to see friends, depression.

3. Development of ideas of persecution or of calamity and impending destruction.

4. Development of ideas of greatness, including the thought that one is Christ or in some special way related to God.

5. Development of a fear or an anxiety which persists apart from external circumstances which might give rise to it.

6. Furious overactivity including sleeplessness.

7. Daydreaming, silliness, increasing inability to care for oneself.

When any of these conditions appear in a parishioner we ought to seek for him, through his family or by personal counsel, an examination by a qualified psychiatrist. To this end an immediate contact we should establish when we enter a new parish is one with a qualified psychiatrist in the vicinity whom we can recommend to our people. To discover such a man we should visit at once our nearest church hospital to discuss their resources in this field. We may also visit a near-by state institution for the care of the insane and ask for recommendations. We may also write to the Council for Clinical Training for advice.

Psychiatric specialists are located almost exclusively in cities, most of them in large metropolitan areas. A careful study of the North Indiana Conference of The Methodist Church disclosed that the average distance from a church to the nearest psychiatrist was twenty-nine miles. Mental health clinics, school counselors, and psychiatric social workers are almost universally urban species. If the benefits which such specialized psychotherapeutic institutions and resources can give to troubled people are to be extended to town and country folk in distress, it will be because the pastor is sufficiently trained to recognize their needs and sufficiently concerned to make contacts with and referral to these agencies.

All this is somewhat far afield from pastoral counseling. But in cases of severe mental illness the dangers inherent in pastoral meddling are so serious as to require this warning before any discussion of pastoral counseling is entered upon. Any action which delays the bringing of medically qualified help to the mentally distressed only serves to make the work of their restoration more difficult and the outcome of their disease more doubtful.

The pastor who wishes to work intensively with individuals who have emotional tensions should realize that such work cannot be done on a hit-or-miss incidental basis. It requires special planning if it is to be helpful in any comprehensive sense. First of all, the pastor should set aside a certain regular period of time for counseling and should make this fact known to his people. Second, he should have a set place which he regularly uses for interviews preferably not the parsonage.

Against the use of the parsonage for counseling is the fact that it is the family home, and it is unfair in particular to a family including children to expect them to contribute to the quiet and the freedom from interference which counseling regularly entails. Some pastors in rural communities either have an office in the church or use a part of the church auditorium for interviews. Others are able to get an office in a store or office building in the village center at which their people trade. The latter arrangement is superior since it is bound to be central and accessible to all the people of a circuit or parish.

The importance of centrality and accessibility is illustrated in the case of the man whose wife is seriously ill and has to be brought to the doctor's office in the village for treatment each week. He needs to talk to his pastor about his fears for her, but there is scarcely time to do so if he must leave his wife at the doctor's office and then drive five miles out into the country to the parsonage. But suppose his pastor's office is less than a block from the doctor's. In that case it is the most natural thing in the world to slip over to the office and unburden himself.

The same argument applies to the man in town to see his lawyer, to seek aid of the welfare authorities, to talk with the banker about his inability to meet his mortgage payment, or to the woman who brings her child to the hospital or visits her husband in jail. The pastor who has arranged for an office central to the business district of his town-country community will find that the natural interplay of economic and social forces will bring his parishioners to his desk for counsel.

There are certain standard requirements for a room that is to be used for counseling interviews. It should be as pleasant and friendly a room as possible; the cold and formal atmosphere of an office is to be avoided. It should have two doors, one to serve as entrance and another as exit so that persons can leave after an interview without having to face others who may be waiting to see the pastor. There should be some vestibule or waiting room available in which persons can wait comfortably if the pastor is busy when they call, and this waiting room should be supplied with a good collection of up-to-date religious books and magazines. The interview room should be so arranged that the pastor sits facing the doorway through which people enter and the person being interviewed sits with his back to the doorway. With this arrangement someone coming into the waiting room for an appointment may open the door, see that the pastor is occupied, and be asked to wait, without intruding upon the person with whom the pastor is then conversing. It is a wise practice to insure privacy in this fashion rather than by locked doors. If persons know that the door is always open so that anyone can look in and yet privacy is effectually guaranteed for emotional expression, any criticism or embarrassment to pastor or parishioner will be avoided. The foregoing arrangement of the interviewing room will help the pastor to guide his own appointments while he maintains privacy for counseling.

When the preliminary plans are made, the pastor should announce through the church bulletin or in his church services: "Many of you have wanted to see me and haven't felt free just to come at any time because you thought I might be busy. As you know, I try to get into every church home at regular intervals but sometimes you want to see me at a time when I'm not calling in your end of town. To provide an opportunity for you to reach me, I'm setting aside Wednesday afternoon from 1:00 to 5:30 for interviews. During those hours I'll be at the church study and anyone is welcome to drop in. When you come, open the door and look in. If I'm visiting with someone else, sit down and wait and I'll see you as soon as I can." See that this announcement is made not once but regularly, preferably posted somewhere so that knowledge of your availability is open to strangers in the community as well as your regular parishioners.

Just an announcement of this kind, however, will not bring people thronging to your study. Some pastors, after sitting alone for a series of afternoons, have given the whole idea up because they felt their people were not interested. Something more positive must be done to bring people in. One of the simplest expedients is to suggest to specific individuals that they come to see you during your appointment hours. The women's society president speaks to you after church and says that she would like to talk to you about committee appointments for next year. It is easy to say to her, "Sister Smith, why don't you drop in to see me at the office Wednesday afternoon when I'll be there, and we can have time to talk thoughtfully about the matter." Or the boy leading the youth fellowship next Sunday evening can be invited to come in to go over the program. Thus through the routine administration of the church program we develop in parishioners the habit of dropping in on Wednesday afternoons to see the pastor. Then when a really serious personal and emotional problem presents itself, the same persons turn naturally to Wednesday afternoon and the pastor at the church office.

Such a procedure also helps the pastor to meet the problem he so often faces in connection with a call or interview in which he discovers that his parishioner needs something which he does not have time or opportunity to give. Perhaps the pastor needs to see that person alone, away from his family. Or perhaps after an hour and a half of visiting the parishioner is worn out yet afraid to let his pastor go. Under such circumstances we do not need to terminate the interview in a way that may seem to close the door of help to a person in need. We can say, "We're both tired now and need to take fresh time to thrash this out. I'm regularly in my office on Wednesday afternoon. Why not come to see me at three o'clock then? We can have half an hour together without interruption, and both of us will have fresh perspective by that time."

A glance at the bibliography will indicate how many resources there are to help the pastor develop skill in the counseling process. Here we are concerned only to relate the counseling process to the total work of the minister. Counseling is not preaching; it is listening rather than telling, accepting people and thus helping them to accept themselves rather than judging or condemning them. But it is very closely related to preaching. The understanding of human nature and its predicaments which we show in our sermons, particularly in the illustrations we use, will bring people to us. Yet here there is a great danger. Never use the story of someone who has counseled with you as a sermon illustration, no matter how excellent it may be, unless the individual has given his permission. Try to disguise the story as we will, we are in danger of disclosing some detail which reveals the person; or, at best, we set speculation going in the parish. Furthermore, we discourage other persons from coming to see us since they feel we might use them as sermon fodder next time. The best procedure so far as intimate material is concerned is to cull our illustrations from the literature of psychology and from fiction and drama.

Counseling is not a matter of a single interview. It almost inevitably involves a series of interviews over a long period of time. Frequent short interviews are better than infrequent prolonged ones. A half hour in general is a pretty good limit for time spent profitably together, though on occasion the interview may need to run beyond that; a persistent refusal on the part of a parishioner to accept the time limitation is an indication of unwillingness to come to grips with reality and must be treated as such. Coming promptly when a definite appointment has been made and leaving promptly are hopeful indications of a developing mature attitude.

The pastor needs always to remember wherein his role is different from that of a psychotherapist. To begin with, the pastor has an ideal of personality—something the psychotherapist may not have at all or only to a limited extent. This ideal is Christ; our purpose is to help men to accept his Spirit and to live by it. It may seem at first blush that this is in conflict with what we have previously said about accepting people rather than condemning them. But to accept people and their acts does not mean that we are to condone or approve those acts. Acceptance often means receiving a man in spite of what he has done rather than by ignoring what he has done. Men who have violated our moral code do not want to be told that their violations are unimportant—they know better than that. They want to be told that there is a way of dealing with a life which has violated the moral law which redeems that life. In other words, they want the gospel message of a God who loves us as we are in order that we may be what he intended us to be.

Again the pastor not only has a gospel, he is a gospel. One of his most significant roles is to be an example of the kind of joyous life his people want to lead. He must always remember that as important as what he says or does for his people is what he is to them. They must see in him a man who overcomes temptation, rises above discouragement, is able to face and meet opposition without bitterness, and who discovers a new zest and joy in each new day. The psychotherapist divorces his life from the daily life of his patients. He is an expert dealing with their problems but not otherwise related to them. The pastor is always related to his people as a leader, winning and wooing them forward by what he is as well as what he does.

Finally, in contrast to the psychotherapist the pastor has a church. In his ministry to persons he has a series of smaller and larger groups and a number of dedicated individuals who stand ready to assist him in his ministry to stricken persons. The psychotherapist may have a social work or clinical organization to assist him, but he never has all the love and devotion bound up in the fellowship of the Church. Early in his ministry the pastor will do well to cultivate two or three fine families in his church who will, when called upon by the pastor, invite a stranger home for Sunday dinner or for an evening of fun without asking any questions at all. And, if he will look for them, he will always find leaders in the women's society and youth fellowship who can be counted upon to open the doors of a rich fellowship to persons lonely and in need.

And behind the Church there stands always the Lord of the Church. To be sure, his divine laws of healing and growth operate for the psychiatrist and the psychotherapist as well as for the pastor. But nowhere are the divine resources of health more readily available than in the fellowship in which their Author is recognized and consciously obeyed. The Master Healer of tortured and fearful minds empowers his ministers in our day to continue his work of healing; and the joyful benediction of his ministry is upon us.

18

Church Administration as
Christian Experience

AT THIS POINT it may seem that the empirical has been stressed so exclusively in these pages as to make the church nothing more than buildings, budgets, and boards.

This reaction is one commonly made not only to books on church administration but to the work of the modern church itself. Many a pastor struggling with committees and quotas says to himself or to his neighbor pastor: "This is not the gospel. I was not called into the ministry to save quotas or to build committees but to save souls and to build the Kingdom. Here I am so busy doing the chores of the church that I have no time for being a Christian minister." There seems to be some grounds for criticism of the church on this matter since at the same time that we have succeeded in making a higher proportion of Americans than ever before members of some church, we have been multiplying evidence that the moral integrity of individuals and the nation is seriously and critically disrupted.

An obvious solution to the matter is that the minister should limit himself to spiritual matters and leave the practical affairs of the church and the world to others. To suggest such a solution is at once to guarantee its rejection by American churchmen, clergy and lay. However critical we may be of the social gospel and however impractical laymen may feel their pastors to be, we are in solid agreement on the basic principle that the Christian spirit and everyday life should go hand in hand. We do not want a separation of religion and life that makes the one impractical and the other unredeemed.

We may vary as to what a redeemed practical life involves; but all of us, ministers and laymen, want that kind of life for ourselves and all people.

Perhaps the difficulty of the ministers who rebel against quotas, and equally the difficulty of the reader of these pages who feels the work is too empirical, is that we have held an untenable division of life in our church planning. We ministers have felt that preaching and pastoring our people constituted the great object of our call and that the details of parish life such as building, budgets, and boards were the necessary chore work of churchmanship to be taken care of as expeditiously as possible. Our laymen, taking their cue from us, have felt that their participation in such matters was not religiously significant and, desiring to render a Christian service, have been impatient at what we have asked them to do.

Suppose for a moment we try another point of view. What if the administration of the church is seen to offer to minister and laymen an opportunity for experience in Christian living? We talk about being Christian in business; is not church business a good place to begin? We talk about settling differences in the spirit of Christ; does that spirit have possible application in a committee meeting? Suppose that a pastor looked upon the suggestions in the preceding pages not as tricks to get an unpleasant job over quickly, but as means whereby a Christian group could do the work of their church in a spirit expressive of its Lord. Then the business affairs of a parish would take on their proper perspective as opportunities for experience in Christian discipleship.

We seldom fail to begin a board or committee meeting with prayer. Suppose we regarded that opportunity to pray with our fellow churchmen as important as family devotions at home. Suppose that rather than uttering a nominal and conventional prayer we gave over the first several minutes of the meeting to a praying together for which we had made the same careful preparation that we use in our Sunday pastoral prayers. Such a functional use of prayer would open channels of divine grace in our own individual lives and in the com-

161

mon life of the committee. No pastor who participated in a board meeting in that vein could feel that he was engaged in anything but the prosecution of his high calling.

Pastors have much to say to their people about a Christian regard for truth. We quote freely the passage from John: "Ye shall know the truth, and the truth shall make you free." Yet often in a business meeting when questions are raised about some pet project of our own, we begin to sulk and act as if to raise questions was to call in question our ministerial honor. A board meeting might be an occasion on which our people learned how deeply we yearn for truth, how ready we are to have our plans called in question and studied in order that truth may be known. If our people could begin to feel that we were not maneuvering to secure a parliamentary majority and a favorable vote but that we were honestly concerned that the truth might prevail, their attention to our preachments on the power of truth and to their own truthfulness would increase.

One of the most important insights of Jesus teaches us that we ought to have regard for every man, that man as man has claim upon us. We preachers are fond of pointing to the mechanical nature of our modern civilization and to the damage it does to the soul of the individual. We argue that man has become a cog in the machine, a number on the assembly line, a replaceable unit in the productive enterprise; whereas God made him his son, and we ought so to treat him. What an opportunity we have in the business life of the church to give an example of how every man may be regarded and treated as worthy in his own right.

Here, for example, is the difficult man on the finance committee. He is always delaying action by raising questions which others do not regard as germane. His conduct consistently indicates an obtuseness to the feelings of his fellows and a blindness to other points of view out of which he needs to grow into Christian maturity. Our disposition often is to bottle up such a man, to contain him until we are in a position deftly to slip him off the committee. But that sort of treatment is only returning to him the obtuseness and blindness which he extends to others. He will never grow under such tutelage and neither will his minister or the other members of the finance committee. Now finance committeemen are busy people, I grant, and their time ought to be conserved; but are they too busy to work with Christ in the redemption of a human soul? It may well be that the main achievement of the finance committee in a single year will be the Christian growth of its most difficult member. The minister who takes the lead in seeing that that member gets a hearing, not only for what he says but for what he is trying to say, will win the following of his finance committee members as he can in no other way. Moreover, if our laymen learn that in any meeting we attend there is always time to be Christian, they will begin to recognize the practical possibilities of Christian discipleship in their own business and personal lives.

Jesus again and again reiterated with his disciples the importance of accepting and tolerating differences. We are to love our enemies, to bless those who curse us, to pray for those who despitefully use us and persecute us. It is very easy for us to apply these counsels to our international opponents but to be completely unforgiving and lacking of understanding toward members of the official board with whom we differ. What an opportunity the business life of the church gives us to practice a wide and Christian tolerance. Is it possible to love and cherish people with whom we sharply differ? Well, if it cannot be done within the fellowship of the church, it is not likely to be done anywhere else. In our day nothing attacks the life of the church so viciously as the attempt of certain interests in church life to exclude from the church persons who have economic or social views opposed to their own. It is doubtless true that in the perfect Kingdom we shall all agree, because we shall all know the truth; but in our very limited and finite churches tolerance of difference and understanding love among men of widely differing viewpoints is the way of redemption and peace. In the long run in the affairs of the church we can and must learn to have more concern for other persons than for our own opinions.

Viewed in this light, church administration becomes a laboratory for the educational and worship life of the church. Here we try the tentative experiments which may in God's good day release creative powers that will redeem the world. Here we practice the virtues and graces of Christian charity in which alone lies man's hope. Once the town and country pastor sees that the life of budgets and boards is a life in which Christian experience may find its focus, he will bring to these administrative activities the same enthusiasm that characterizes his other ministries.

The Church and the world have long accepted the goal of Jesus. The Kingdom of which he preached is regarded as a worthy dream even by the cynic who despairs of its achievement. But the world has never and the Church has only hesitantly accepted the method of Jesus. It is hard even for churchmen to see that he regarded his Kingdom as a present possibility of attitude and fellowship and not as some Utopia in a distant tomorrow. There are certain laws governing the movement of physical objects. These laws will operate at the official board meeting next Monday night. There are other laws of organic growth which will operate there as well. The psychological laws of learning and the sociologically defined laws of role-playing and status will also apply Monday night; and we may, perhaps, be more conscious of these than of those previously mentioned. Monday night another order of law may be ours, the law of the Kingdom. The Kingdom is among us, its law is written in us; but it is the law of freedom and governs us only as we accept it. The day is speedily coming when pastor and people will go to the board meeting Monday night as Christians and find the joy of their salvation and the peace of his Kingdom in their fellowship.

A P P E N D I X

The LaGrange, Indiana, Larger Parish Council serves as an example of the importance and value of developing a council through which several churches within the same community area can express their essential religious and social unity. The following constitution and bylaws—approved September 8, 1948, at the Mongo Methodist Church—are those under which this council operates.

The LaGrange County Larger Parish Council

CONSTITUTION

ARTICLE I

The name of this organization shall be known as the LaGrange County Larger Parish Council.

ARTICLE II

The purpose of the council shall be to exalt Christ throughout the LaGrange community area.

To be able to do this the council shall:

1. Survey and study the total community area.
2. After careful study establish the policy of the parish.
3. Plan meetings that can be carried out co-operatively that will aid in the enrichment of the spiritual, economic, civic, and social life of the persons living within the LaGrange community area.
4. Welcome and receive churches of any recognized denomination that wish to co-operate in the Larger Parish program by:
   a) Appointing representatives to the council.
   b) Attending council and parish meetings.
   c) Giving moral and spiritual support to the parish program.
   d) Furnishing adequate financial support to the total parish program.
5. Provide for adequate committees to carry out parish policy effectively.

165

In general the parish shall seek to place the resources of the Methodist Church at the disposal of each co-operating church within the parish.

ARTICLE III

Membership in this council shall consist of one representative elected by the official board, one representative elected by the woman's organization, one representative elected by the youth organization, and the Sunday-school superintendent of each member church. The pastors, the charge lay leader, and the central treasurer of the parish shall be members of the council.

ARTICLE IV

The officers of this council shall be president, vice-president, secretary, and treasurer. The officers shall assume office at the first regular meeting following their election and serve for a period of one year or until their successors are elected. The pastors shall not be elected to an office of the council.

ARTICLE V

The members of the council shall act as the board of directors of the LaGrange County Larger Parish.

ARTICLE VI

The election of officers shall be held at the annual meeting, which shall be the regular June meeting.

ARTICLE VII

The LaGrange County Larger Parish of the Methodist Church shall be made up of the following member churches: Bethel, East Springfield, Lakeview, Plato, Mongo, and Valentine.

ARTICLE VIII

Amendments to this constitution can be made only after the amendment or amendments are proposed at a regular meeting, notice of the proposed amendment or amendments sent to each member church of the parish and to each council member. Voting then shall be made at the next regular meeting of the council. Voting shall be by ballot.

To pass an amendment it shall require a majority vote of the members of the council present at the meeting when the amendment or amendments are voted upon.

BYLAWS

SECTION I

The council shall have one regular meeting each month. Special meetings may be called by the president of the council or by one third of the council after proper written notice has been given. Notice must be given at least five days before date of called meeting.

SECTION II

The nomination of officers of the council shall be made by a nominating committee and at least three nominations shall be presented for each office. Also, additional nominations shall be called for from the floor at the meeting when the election is held. Those who are members of the council are the only ones eligible to vote or hold office in the council.

The nominating committee shall present the names of nominees for one office at a time. After voting for that office has been finished then the nominations for the next office are to be presented.

SECTION III

The duties of the president shall be to act as chairman of all regular and special meetings of the council. He shall be the spokesman for the council whenever a representative is needed outside of the regular or special meetings. He shall call any special meetings when he feels the matter or matters to be discussed are important enough to require special attention. He shall take into consideration any request from other members of the council for a special meeting and act in the best interest of the parish. He shall appoint committees specified by the council.

The duties of the vice-president shall be to assume the duties of the president in the president's absence.

The duties of the secretary shall be to keep an accurate and faithful record of all activities of the council. He shall give notice of any special meetings to the proper persons. He shall conduct any correspondence necessary for the business of the council. He shall keep an accurate roll of the members of the council.

The duties of the treasurer shall be to keep an accurate account of all funds paid in to pastoral support, apportionments, and world service by the member churches and individuals and to disburse the same.

SECTION IV

At the first election each church shall elect one representative for one year, one representative for two years, and one representative for three years. Thereafter each church shall elect one new member each year for a three year term.

SECTION V

Vacancies shall be filled by an election of a new member by the group represented.

Any vacancy of a parish office shall be filled by an election from the members of the council, after the proper notice has been given.

SECTION VI

A quorum shall be no less than four member churches represented at the council meeting, or 10 (ten) council members.

SECTION VII

The personnel of a council committee: A majority of the members of a committee responsible to the council must be members of the council.

SECTION VIII

The parliamentary authority shall be *Robert's Rules of Order*.

SECTION IX

Amendments to these bylaws can be made only after the amendment or amendments are proposed at a regular meeting, notice of the proposed amendment or amendments sent to each church of the parish and to each council member. Voting shall be made at the next regular meeting of the council. Voting shall be by ballot.

To pass an amendment it shall require a majority vote of the members of the council present at the meeting when the amendment it voted upon.

BIBLIOGRAPHY

Chapter I. "The Uniqueness of the Town and Country Church"

General Rural Church Administration

Blackwood, Andrew W. *Pastoral Leadership.* New York and Nashville: Abingdon-Cokesbury Press, 1949.

Boisen, Anton T. *Problems in Religion and Life.* New York and Nashville: Abingdon-Cokesbury Press, 1946.

Gebhard, Anna Laura. *Rural Parish!* New York and Nashville: Abingdon-Cokesbury Press, 1947.

————. *Parsonage Doorway.* New York and Nashville: Abingdon-Cokesbury Press, 1950.

Herzel, Frank B. *More Than Bread.* Philadelphia: Muhlenberg Press, 1950.

Hewitt, Arthur W. *Highland Shepherds.* Chicago: Willett, Clark & Co., 1939.

————. *God's Back Pasture.* Chicago: Willett, Clark & Co., 1941.

Randolph, H. S., and Maloney, Alice. *A Manual for Town and Country Churches.* New York: Dept. of Rural Church of the Board of National Missions, Presbyterian Church, U. S. A., 1950.

Richardson, Harry V. *Dark Glory.* New York: Friendship Press, 1947.

Evangelistic Methods

Bryan, Dawson C. *A Workable Plan of Evangelism.* New York and Nashville: Abingdon-Cokesbury Press, 1945.

————. *A Handbook of Evangelism for Laymen.* New York and Nashville: Abingdon-Cokesbury Press, 1948.

Meckel, Aaron N. *New Day for Evangelism.* New York: E. P. Dutton & Co., Inc., 1947.

Munro, Harry C. *Fellowship Evangelism Through Church Groups.* St. Louis: Bethany Press, 1951.

Chapter II. "The Town and Country Minister"

Felton, Ralph A. *The Rural Parsonage.* Madison, N. J.: Drew University, N. J.

Harmon, Nolan B. *Ministerial Ethics and Etiquette.* New York and Nashville: Abingdon-Cokesbury Press, 1950.

Leiffer, Murray H. *The Layman Looks at the Minister.* New York and Nashville: Abingdon-Cokesbury Press, 1947.

Mueller, Frederick F., and Hartshorne, Hugh. *Ethical Dilemmas of Ministers.* New York: Charles Scribner's Sons, 1937.

Chapter III. "The Minister's Schedule"

May, Mark A. *The Profession of the Ministry,* Vol. II of *The Education of American Ministers.* New York: Institute of Social and Religious Research, 1934.

Palmer, Albert W. *The Minister's Job.* New York: Harper & Brothers, 1949.

Quayle, William A. *The Pastor-Preacher.* New York and Cincinnati: The Methodist Book Concern, 1927.

Spann, J. Richard, ed. *The Ministry.* New York and Nashville: Abingdon-Cokesbury Press, 1949.

Chapter IV. "The Parish Structure"

Brunner, Edmund deS. *The Larger Parish: A Movement or an Enthusiasm?* New York: Institute of Social and Religious Research, 1934.

Rich, Mark. *The Larger Parish,* Bull. 408. Ithaca, N. Y.: New York State College of Agriculture of Cornell University, 1939.

Smith, Rockwell C. *The Church in Our Town.* New York and Nashville: Abingdon-Cokesbury Press, 1945.

Chapter V. "The Parish Program"

Crossland, Weldon. *A Planned Program for the Church Year.* New York and Nashville: Abingdon-Cokesbury Press, 1951.

Maves, Paul B., and Cedarleaf, J. Lennart. *Older People and the Church.* New York and Nashville: Abingdon-Cokesbury Press, 1949.

Chapter VI. "Planning the Parish Budget"

Cashman, Robert C. *The Business Administration of a Church.* Chicago: Willett, Clark & Co., 1937.

———. *The Finances of a Church.* New York: Harper & Brothers, 1949.

Chapter VII. "Raising the Parish Budget"

Canvasser's Handbook. New York: Committee on Every-Member Canvass, Presbyterian Church in the U.S.A., n.d.

Crossland, Weldon Matthews, E. J., and Nease, Edgar H. *How to Organize and Conduct the Every Member Canvass.* Chicago: World Service Agencies of the Methodist Church, n.d.

Felton, Ralph A. *The Lord's Acre.* New York: Division of Home Missions and Church Extension, The Methodist Church, 1946.

BIBLIOGRAPHY

Chapter VIII. "Spreading the Parish News"
Brodie, W. Austin. *Keeping Your Church in the News.* New York:
Fleming H. Revell Co., 1942.
Fortson, John L. *How to Make Friends for Your Church.* New
York: Association Press, 1943.
Harral, Stewart. *Public Relations for Churches.* New York and
Nashville: Abingdon-Cokesbury Press, 1945.
Parker, Everett C. *Religious Radio.* New York: Harper & Brothers,
1948.
Wolseley, Roland E. *Interpreting the Church Through Press and
Radio.* Philadelphia: Muhlenberg Press, 1951.

Chapter IX. "Housing the Church"
Conover, Elbert M. *The Church Builder.* New York: Interdenomina-
tional Bureau of Architecture, 1948.
Murphy, Bonneau P. *The Building and Care of Methodist Church
Property.* New York: Board of Missions, The Methodist Church,
1951.
Webber, Frederick R. *The Small Church.* Cleveland: J. H. Jansen,
1937.
Whitman, Roger C. *Church Maintenance Manual.* New York:
Doubleday & Co., 1951.

Chapter X. "Principles and Pattern in Parish Worship"
Palmer, Albert W. *The Art of Conducting Public Worship.* New
York: The Macmillan Co., 1939.
———. *Come, Let Us Worship.* New York: The Macmillan Co., 1941.
Ziegler, Edward K. *A Book of Worship for Village Churches.* New
York: Agricultural Missions Foundation, 1939.
———. *Rural People at Worship.* New York: Agricultural Missions,
Inc., 1943.

Chapter XI. "Means of Grace in Parish Worship"
Gibson, George M. *The Story of the Christian Year.* New York and
Nashville: Abingdon-Cokesbury Press, 1945.
Heimsath, Charles H. *The Genius of Public Worship.* New York:
Charles Scribner's Sons, 1944.
McCutchan, Robert G. *Our Hymnody.* New York and Nashville:
Abingdon-Cokesbury Press, 1937.
Stafford, Thomas A. *Christian Symbolism in the Evangelical Churches.*
New York and Nashville: Abingdon-Cokesbury Press, 1942.

Poetry
Auslander, Joseph, and Hill, Frank E., eds. *The Winged Horse
Anthology.* New York: Doubleday, Doran & Co., 1929.

Carman, Bliss, ed. *Oxford Book of American Verse*. New York: Oxford University Press, 1927.

Kreymborg, Alfred, ed. *Lyric America*. New York: Coward-McCann, 1930.

Quiller-Couch, Arthur, ed. *Oxford Book of English Verse*. New York: Oxford University Press, 1939.

Untermeyer, Louis, ed. *The New Modern American & British Poetry*. New York: Harcourt, Brace and Company, 1949.

Chapter XII. "Sacraments in Church Worship"

Blackwood, Andrew W. *The Fine Art of Public Worship*. New York and Nashville: Abingdon-Cokesbury Press, 1939.

Ziegler, Edward K. *Rural People at Worship*. New York: Agricultural Missions, Inc., 1943.

Chapter XIII. "Rites in Church Worship"

Blackwood, Andrew W. *The Funeral*. Philadelphia: Westminster Press, 1942.

Brand, Norton F., and Ingram, V. M. *The Pastor's Legal Adviser*. New York and Nashville: Abingdon-Cokesbury Press, 1942.

Post, Emily. *Etiquette*. New York: Funk & Wagnalls Co., 1931.

Woods, Marjorie. *Your Wedding, How to Plan and Enjoy It*. Indianapolis: Bobbs-Merrill Co., 1942.

Chapter XIV. "The Pastor's Ministry in the Home"

Blackwood, Andrew W. *Pastoral Work; A Source Book for Ministers*. Philadelphia: Ryerson Press, 1945.

Chapter XV. "The Pastor's Ministry to the Sick"

Cabot, Richard C., and Dicks, Russell L. *The Art of Ministering to the Sick*. New York: The Macmillan Co., 1936.

Mott, Frederick D., and Roemer, Milton I. *Rural Health and Medical Care*. New York: McCraw-Hill Book Co., 1948.

Wise, Carroll A. *Religion in Illness and Health*. New York: Harper & Brothers, 1942.

Chapter XVI. "The Pastor's Ministry to the Bereaved" There is, unfortunately, no book dealing specifically with the pastor and the bereaved. Blackwood in *The Funeral* and Wise in *Pastoral Counseling; Its Theory and Practice* give helpful observations.

Chapter XVII. "The Pastor's Ministry as Counselor"

Dicks, Russell L. *Pastoral Work and Personal Counseling*. New York: The Macmillan Co., 1949.

172

Hiltner, Seward. *Pastoral Counseling.* New York and Nashville: Abingdon-Cokesbury Press, 1949.
Wise, Carroll A. *Pastoral Counseling; Its Theory and Practice.* New York: Harper & Brothers, 1951.

Chapter XVIII. "Church Administration as Christian Experience"
Edwards, Richard H. *A Person-minded Ministry.* New York and Nashville: Abingdon-Cokesbury Press, 1940.
Seifert, Harvey. *The Church in Community Action.* New York and Nashville: Abingdon-Cokesbury Press, 1952.

INDEX